BLOSSOMS
OF THE
DHARMA

BLOSSOMS OF THE DHARMA

LIVING AS A BUDDHIST NUN

EDITED BY

THUBTEN CHODRON

North Atlantic Books
Berkeley, California

Blossoms of the Dharma: Living as a Buddhist Nun

Published by
North Atlantic Books
P.O. Box 12327
Berkeley, California 94712

Cover and book design by Joan Stepp Smith
Cover photograph by John C. McDougall. Used with permission from the Tibetan Nun's Project.

Printed in the United States of America

Blossoms of the Dharma: Living as a Buddhist Nun is sponsored by the Society for the Study of Native Arts and Sciences, a nonprofit educational corporation whose goals are to develop an educational and crosscultural perspective linking various scientific, social, and artistic fields; to nurture a holistic view of arts, sciences, humanities, and healing; and publish and distribute literature on the relationship of mind, body, and nature.

Library of Congress Cataloging-in-Publication Data

Blossoms of the dharma: living as a Buddhist nun / edited by Thubten Chodron.
  p. cm.
ISBN 1-55643-325-5 (alk. paper)
  1. Buddhist nuns—Religious life. 2. Monasticism and religious orders for women, Buddhist. I. Thubten Chodron, 1950-

BQ6150 B56 1999   99-043221
294.3'657 21-dc21   CIP

1 2 3 4 5 6 / 03 02 01 00 99

THUBTEN CHODRON, HIS HOLINESS THE DALAI LAMA, TENZIN PALMO, TENZIN YONTEN AT DHARAMSALA, INDIA

CONTENTS

THE NUNS' TEACHING

APPENDICES

MESSAGE

Shakyamuni Buddha attained enlightenment in Bodhgaya over two and a half thousand years ago, yet his teaching remains refreshing and relevant today. No matter who we are or where we live, we all want happiness and dislike suffering. The Buddha recommended that in working to overcome suffering, we should help others as much as we can. He futher advised that if we cannot actually be of help, we should at least be careful not to harm anyone.

Part of Buddhist practice involves training our minds through meditation. But if our training in calming our minds, developing qualities like love, compassion, generosity and patience, is to be effective, we must put them into practice in day to day life. In an increasingly interdependent world our own welfare and happiness depend on many other people. As human beings others have right to peace and happiness equal to our own. We therefore have a responsibility to help those in need.

This conference is mainly focused on the concerns of Buddhist nuns. In the past, in many Buddhist countries, nuns did not have the same educational opportunities as monks, nor access to the same facilities. Due to prevailing social attitudes nuns were often treated or regarded in ways that are no longer acceptable today. I am happy to see that these things are beginning to change. Recently, the first winter Debate Session for nuns was held in Dharamsala, in which nuns from several nunneries participated successfully. Here was clear evidence of the improved educational standards that nuns now enjoy.

Throughout history there have been individual nuns who rose to eminence, beginning of course with Mahaprajapati. Whatever other qualities they may have had, these women revealed remarkable determination and courage. They were single-minded in pursuit of their chosen goal, without regard for encouragement or disappointment. I urge you, both as individuals and communities, to adopt a similar approach. I believe that inner peace plays an important role in the development of determination and courage. In that state of mind you can face difficulties with calm and reason, while keeping your inner happiness. In my experience, the Buddha's teachings of love, kindness and tolerance, the conduct of nonviolence, and especially the view that all things are relative and interdependent are a source of that inner peace.

I have remarked before that whenever Buddhism has taken root in a new land there has always been a certain variation in the style in which it is observed. The Buddha himself taught differently according to the place, the occasion, and the situation of those who were listening to him. To some extent, as Buddhist nuns, you are now participating in the evolution of a Buddhism for a new time, a time when the universal principle of the equality of all human beings takes precedence. It is heartening to observe, as your conference clearly demonstrates, that Buddhist women are casting off traditional and outmoded restraints.

All of you have a great responsibility to take the essence of Buddhism and put it into practice in your own lives. Having taken ordination we must constantly remember that the primary reason for holding vows as a nun or a monk is to be able to dedicate ourselves to the practice of the Dharma. Even if only a few individuals try to create mental peace and happiness within themselves and act responsibly and kind-heartedly towards others, they will have a positive influence in their community. As well as being equally capable, women have an equal responsibility to do this.

I offer my greetings to all participants, as well as my sincere prayers that your conference may be successful in contributing to a more peaceful and happier world.

January 12, 1996

FOREWORD

I MET VENERABLE THUBTEN CHODRON WHEN WE WERE SUITE-MATES AT A
LARGE HOTEL, SOME YEARS AGO, ALONG WITH THREE OTHER WOMEN
PRESENTERS AT A WEEK-LONG BUDDHIST CONFERENCE. I was touched that
her being a nun did not create a sense of separation from the rest of us—we
were all women devoted to practicing and teaching the Dharma, and all of
us enjoyed an easy delight in meeting and being with each other. I was
inspired to realize that, notwithstanding the intensity of the conference all
day and our hours of conversation at night, Chodron was up long before
anyone else doing her morning prayer practice. She clearly loved the life
she had chosen and could gracefully interpolate it into the life she shared
with all of us.

Monks and nuns, people who dedicate their entire lives to practicing
and teaching the Dharma and to living the renunciant lifestyle, are symbolic
of the path to which all Dharma students are committed. The Buddha
taught the method for transforming the heart through this special structure
for training the mind and serving others. We lay people assume that special
structure and discipline during meditation retreats. It is important to have
people in our community who take it on for a lifetime. We need monastics
at our core.

The teachers at Spirit Rock Meditation Center in Marin County,
California are lay teachers, and our students are men and women of all
ages, from many social and cultural communities, including people with
enduring connections with other faith traditions. In July of 1998, at Spirit
Rock's opening day ceremony, Ajahn Amaro, a Theravadin monk and our
friend and neighbor, lead the procession of teachers into the meditation

hall as we all chanted homage to the Buddha. His doing this was important to our teaching faculty and meaningful to everyone.

The potential influence of Buddhist nuns and monks is much wider than just our own community. Recently I noticed the cover story of a well-known business weekly magazine was "Is Greed Good for You?" I was sure the title was a joke and the story would be a values reminder, so I read the article and was dismayed to find that it was serious. Thinking of this book of nun's stories, I know that in a culture believing consumerism and materialism to be the source of happiness, the visible presence of renunciants in the society is an important reminder. It is a teaching in itself. Ancient texts tell us of King Asoka who had led his people in a terrible battle in which many were slain. The following morning, as he surveyed the scene of the conflict, King Asoka also noticed the serene, peaceful presence of a Buddhist monk. Seeing him, Asoka regretted the violence and was moved to become a student of Buddhism. In so doing, he converted his entire kingdom and instructed them in wise conduct. My hope is that just as King Asoka's vision converted him to non-hatred, the presence of monastics in our society will serve to convert our culture to non-greed.

Whenever I read historical accounts of Buddhist nuns, I admire their valor. Cultures have not supported women in choosing the renunciant life, and in the Buddhist world, too, their position has generally been secondary to men. It is important for us as modern Buddhists to read these accounts of contemporary women with their goals, hopes, difficulties, and triumphs. They are varied in background, come from all over the world, and span the spectrum of Buddhist lineages; but they all share the passion for a life dedicated to liberation, and their example can inspire all of us in our own practice.

Early in my own meditation practice, I dreamed that I became a nun.

My dream was symbolic, representing my enthusiasm for practice and my hope for awakened understanding. For those women for whom the dream might become reality, we need communities of nuns who study, practice, and teach, and we need the stories of the women in this book to make this choice widely known and available.

SYLVIA BOORSTEIN
FOUNDING TEACHER
SPIRIT ROCK MEDITATION CENTER
WOODACRE, CALIFORNIA

PROLOGUE

AN IMPORTANT CHAPTER IN THE TRANSMISSION OF THE BUDDHA'S TEACHINGS TO THE WEST IS THE DEVELOPMENT OF A BUDDHIST MONASTIC COMMUNITY. The Three Jewels to which one goes for refuge as a Buddhist are the Buddha, his teachings (Dharma), and the spiritual community (Sangha). The latter traditionally refers to the ordained community of nuns and monks. While the sangha has been the center of the Buddhist community in traditional societies, its role in the West is a work in progress.

A small number of Western Buddhists have chosen to ordain as monks and nuns. Giving up the householder life, they take a precept of celibacy, shave their hair, don monastic robes, and enter into what is, in most Buddhist traditions, a lifelong commitment in which their daily activities are guided by the system of precepts know as the Vinaya.

Theirs is a challenging undertaking. On the one hand, they take on the full measure of the Buddhist teachings, accepting the definition of a full-time practitioner offered from within the tradition itself. On the other hand, as Westerners, they enter into a monastic system which has until recently existed only in Asian societies, where the Dharma and its culture are intricately interwoven. In addition, the precepts that guide and structure their lives originated during the time of the Buddha, more than twenty-five hundred years ago. Many of these rules are timeless and relevant; some are difficult to abide by in the modern age. Naturally, questions of modernization and adaptation arise.

Western monastics also face the challenge of entering this life in societies without a pre-existing role or place for women who don Buddhist robes, because Buddhism is not a dominant religion in Western countries. The monks and nuns one sees in Western industrialized countries are Catholic, and the expectation society has about them come out of histories of Catholicism. Western nuns must live creatively, often training in an Asian cultural context and later living among Western mores and values.

Western women have another set of challenges. Although many people can and do make the case that Buddhism is at heart an egalitarian religion in which women's equal potential for enlightenment has never been denied, the actual situation of ordained women has, more often that not, been far less than equal. In fact, in many Buddhist countries women do not, at this time, have the opportunity to receive ordination of the same level as that of men, although such an ordination for women has existed since the time of the Buddha. An important movement in the Buddhist world to change this situation has been spurred in large part by the interest and work of Western women.

This book comes out of a conference at which predominantly Western women from around the world representing a variety of Buddhist traditions met to grapple with these issues, to find ways to refine and improve the choices they have made, to encourage each other, and to become a sangha. What shines through in their voices is the power and force of an ordained life, the fact that despite the difficulties—and for this pioneer generation of Western Buddhist nuns, there are many—the life they have chosen offers a clear and meaningful path of full-time commitment to spiritual endeavor.

Having that choice is important. From their own side, women need the opportunity to choose to devote their lives to spiritual rather than worldly pursuits. Western women who discover Buddhism need to see that this *is* a choice, and a vibrant, socially active, intellectually provocative choice. In our excessively consumerist and materialist culture, the existence of a visible counterbalance is critical. The presence of men and women who choose to focus on spiritual, rather than material, goals confronts and inspires society as a whole. This book offers a meaningful window into their pioneering world.

Elizabeth Napper
Director, Tibetan Nuns Project
Dharamsala, India

PREFACE

Blossoms of the Dharma: Living as a Buddhist Nun grew out of Life as a Western Buddhist Nun, a three-week educational program for nuns held in Bodhgaya, India, in February, 1996. During this course, the nuns listened to teachings on the Vinaya—monastic discipline—from a Tibetan *geshe* and a Chinese bhikshuni, other teachings from a variety of qualified spiritual masters, and talks by the nuns themselves. This volume is a compilation of the latter. These talks were given in a relaxed, friendly atmosphere, generally in the evening at the end of a long, happy day of listening to Vinaya teachings, meditating, and discussing the Dharma. The nuns were eager to share their experiences and learn from each other. Although they were all Buddhist nuns, they came from a wide variety of backgrounds and had trained as nuns in various countries and conditions. Much was to be learned from each other's experiences.

Although this book arises from a specific event, its content extends far beyond that. Here we glimpse the history, discipline, life experiences, and teachings of nuns from a variety of Buddhist traditions. I teach in both the East and the West and have noticed that even before people want to listen to a Dharma talk by a nun, they want to know about her life. What does living as a nun entail? Why did she make that choice? What are her life experiences?

The people who contributed to this volume are all Buddhist practitioners. Although some are also scholars, their main passion is to practice and actualize the Buddha's teachings. Most became nuns in order to commit their lives to this process. These are people whose primary interest is transforming their own minds, and through this to contribute to society and to the welfare of others. They are not people who seek public recognition for their achievements or power in religious institutions, although being human beings, these motivations may of course sneak in at times—and hopefully are counteracted! Most of the contributors are Western nuns, many of whom have lived in other cultures and countries in order to learn and practice the Dharma. By discovering through experience how the Dharma is practiced in monasteries in traditional Buddhist societies, they have a wealth of knowledge and experience to share as they bring the Dharma and the Buddhist monastic tradition to the West. The three Asian contributors help us learn from the grounded experience of well-established Buddhist traditions.

This book begins with the message His Holiness the Dalai Lama sent to *Life as a Western Buddhist Nun*. Here we see clearly the changing role of women in Buddhism. Such a message would not have been written even a few decades ago.

An introduction follows, setting the stage and giving the background about why women, especially those who grew up in modern Western cultures, become Buddhist nuns. Section I of the book discusses the history and monastic discipline (Vinaya) of the nuns and the nuns' order. Due to their scholarship and knowledge about the nuns' history and discipline, Bhikshuni Lekshe Tsomo, Dr. Chatsumarn Kabilsingh, and Bhikshuni Jampa Tsedroen have, for years, been instrumental in improving the situation of nuns all over the world.

Section II presents nuns' experiences and life styles. Bhikshuni Tsultrim Palmo, originally from Poland, tells of Gampo Abbey in Canada, which follows the Nyingma-Kagyu tradition of Tibetan Buddhism. Ajahn Sundara, from the Thai Forest tradition of Theravada Buddhism, tells about the lives of nuns transporting that ancient tradition to the West, and Bhikshuni

Tenzin Namdrol tells of life at Thich Nhat Hanh's community in France, Plum Village. Bhikshuni Ngawang Chodron from the Nyingma tradition of Tibetan Buddhism has lived in monasteries in China and reveals how the nuns there live and train. Sramanerika Thubten Lhatso, from Tibet, relates her experience of training in Tibet, being uprooted, and preserving the nuns' tradition in India. An Australian, Chi-Kwang Sunim tells of living in Korea and training with the Zen nuns there, while Reverend Mitra Bishop tells of the Zen tradition as practiced both in Japan and in the United States.

Section III reveals the teachings of the nuns. I begin by describing how to avoid some easy-to-make mistakes in Dharma practice. Bhikshuni Jampa Chokyi, a Spanish nun from the Gelu tradition of Tibetan Buddhism, discusses how to relate to a spiritual master, and Bhikshuni Wendy Finster, a nun and therapist from Australia, brings a psychological perspective to Dharma practice. Venerable Khandro Rinpoche, a highly respected Tibetan nun and teacher, helps us discover the essence of Dharma practice.

The appendices inform interested readers about the *Life as a Western Buddhist Nun* educational program. The glossary contains words frequently used in this book. Other words which are used only once and whose meanings are clear in that context are not included. A list of further reading offers resources for the topics discussed in this book.

Sanskrit spellings of foreign terms are used by contributors from the Mahayana Buddhist traditions, while Pali spellings are used by those from the Theravada Buddhist traditions. The Sanskrit, Pali, Tibetan, and English equivalents of many terms are found in the glossary. For ease of reading, foreign terms frequently used in this book—such as bhikshuni, sramanerika, and bodhicitta—are not italicized, while ones infrequently used are. For a similar reason, diacritics have been omitted, although these are used in scholarly publications. The term "Sangha" indicates those who have realized emptiness directly and are thus objects of refuge, while "sangha" indicates the community of fully ordained monks or nuns. At times, "he" and "she" are alternated to be gender neutral where appropriate.

Because the vast majority of pieces in this volume began as oral presentations, they were condensed and edited to form the essays contained here. The information and views expressed in each piece are those of the individual contributor and are not necessarily those of the editor. Each nun speaks according to the tradition(s) she studies and practices; explanations of some points may vary from one Buddhist tradition to another.

THANK YOU

Bhikshuni Jampa Chokyi and I, as the organizers of *Life as a Western Buddhist Nun,* wish to offer special thanks to many people. His Holiness the Dalai Lama, Tenzin Geyche Tetong, Bhikshu Lhakdor, Venerable Master Bhikshuni Wu Yin, and Bhikshuni Jenny have been continuously supportive of our endeavors and helpful in accomplishing them. We also thank Venerable Sonam Thabkye, Bhikshuni Jampa Tsedroen, Bhikshuni Lekshe Tsomo, Bhikshuni Tenzin Kacho, Sramanerika Tenzin Dechen, Sramanerika Paloma Alba, Mary Grace Lentz, Margaret Cormier, Bets Greer, Lynn Gebetsberger, Kim Houk, Lydia Kaye Maddux, Sarah Porter, Angel Vannoy, and Karen Shertzer for their tireless efforts before or during the program. We are grateful to Dharma Friendship Foundation in Seattle for enabling us to organize *Life as a Western Buddhist Nun* under their auspices, Luminary Temple in Taiwan, and many other kind benefactors who made this program possible, and to all the participants, who made this program successful.

I would like also to thank those who assisted in the preparation of this book: Barbara Rona for her thoughtful, precise editing of the manuscript;

Lindy Hough, Barbara Rona, and Joan Stigliani for their valuable suggestions; Yeo Soo Hwa and Lorraine Ayre for transcribing the talks; Bets Greer for proofreading the manuscript, and the members of Dharma Friendship Foundation for their support while I worked on this book. I would especially like to thank my wonderful Dharma sisters who gave these informative and inspiring talks for their dedication to the Buddha's teachings and for sharing their knowledge and experience with others.

May our efforts to learn, practice, and spread the Buddha's precious teachings ripen in the temporary and ultimate happiness of each and every sentient being.

Bhikshuni Thubten Chodron
Seattle, U. S. A.
May 30, 1999

Introduction

Bhikshuni Thubten Chodron

W HEN THE FIRST BLOSSOMS APPEAR IN SPRINGTIME, OUR HEARTS ARE UPLIFTED. Each blossom is unique and attracts our attention, generating in us a sense of inspiration and curiosity. In the same way, Buddhist nuns who are dedicated to ethical discipline give us hope and optimism in our materialistic, violent world. Having given up family life and consumerism to devote their lives to Buddhist teachings, or Dharma, they catch our attention. They voluntarily assume precepts—ethical guidelines to train their body, speech, and mind—and abstain from having careers, regular social lives, and intimate physical relationships. Yet these nuns are happy and have a sense of meaning and purpose in life. What are their lives like? *Blossoms of the Dharma: Living as a Buddhist Nun* gives a glimpse of the fascinating world in which they move.

Most of the contributors to this book are Western women who are ordained Buddhist nuns. They are a relatively new phenomenon, the fragrant blossoms of a tradition with ancient roots going back more than twenty-five centuries. This book describes how the nuns' order began and describes some of the reasons women raised in the West wish to become Buddhist monastics in the twentieth century.

THE NUNS' ORDER

Soon after the Buddha's enlightenment, many people were attracted to this serene, wise, and compassionate man and sought to become his disciples. Some became lay followers, maintaining their lives as householders with a family, while others became monks, thus beginning the order of monks.

Five years after this, the order of nuns began. The inspiring story of its origin begins with Mahaprajapati, the Buddha's aunt and stepmother who cared for him as a child. She, together with five hundred women from the Shakya clan, shaved their heads and walked the long distance from Kapilavastu to Vaisali to request ordination. At first the Buddha declined, but after the intercession of his close disciple Ananda, the Buddha confirmed women's ability to attain liberation and began the bhikshuni or full ordination for women. The order of nuns existed and flourished for many centuries in India and spread to other countries as well: Sri Lanka, China, Korea, Vietnam, and so forth. In the twentieth century, many Westerners have become Buddhist, and of those, some have chosen to ordain as monastics.

Buddhism is still new in the West. Dharma centers and temples from a variety of Buddhist traditions exist in most Western countries. Monasteries devoted to study and meditation practice, on the other hand, are fewer, as most monastics tend to live in a Dharma center or temple where they interact with and serve the lay community. Very little research has been done about Buddhist monastics of either Asian or Western origin living in the West, nor are there statistics about the number of monks and nuns. It is a fascinating subject worthy of research. This book presents an introduction to the lives and lifestyles of this new generation of nuns.

WESTERNERS TURNING TO BUDDHISM

In the past four decades, Westerners' knowledge of and interest in Buddhism has increased dramatically. Many factors have contributed to this: for example, improved communication and technology making more information available; improved transportation allowing Asian teachers to come to the West and Westerners to visit Asia; political upheavals driving Asians from their homelands to other countries; the youthful rebellion and curiosity of many baby boomers; and disillusionment with Western religious institutions.

However, beyond these external conditions are internal ones as well. The Western nuns who contributed to this book come from a variety of countries and religions of origin. Some were clearly on a spiritual search, others "stumbled" upon Buddhism. But all of them found meaning in the Buddha's teachings and in Buddhist meditation. In the Buddha's first teaching, he explained the Four Noble Truths: 1) our life is filled with unsatisfactory experiences; 2) these have causes—ignorance, anger, and clinging attachment within our minds; 3) there exists a state free from these—nirvana; and 4) there is a path to eliminate these unsatisfactory experiences and their causes and to attain nirvana. In this way he explained our present situation, as well as our potential, and clearly described a step-by-step path for transforming our minds and hearts. This practical approach, which can be applied in daily life, not just in a temple or church, is attractive to many people in the West. Similarly, meditation, which can be done either alone or in a group, provides a way to understand, accept, and improve ourselves. In addition, meeting realized Asian masters convinced the first generation of Western Buddhists that spiritual transformation is indeed possible. In their talks, some of the nuns share what attracted them to the Dharma, as well as the reasons that led to their ordination.

THE MONASTIC LIFE

Of course, not everyone interested in Buddhism or becoming a Buddhist is interested in becoming a monastic. People have various dispositions and inclinations, and one can practice the Dharma as a lay person as well. In fact, most Buddhists in both Asia and the West remain lay practitioners. Nevertheless, there is a corner in many people's hearts that wonders, "What would it be like to be a monastic?" Even when people decide that monasticism is not a life style suitable for them, it is still valuable for them to understand and appreciate it, because the monastics are a noticeable and important element in the Buddhist community.

If we practice a spiritual path—as a lay person or as a monastic—we clearly have to make certain changes in our daily habits to develop our positive qualities and behaviors and to discourage negative ones. For this reason, the Buddha encouraged us to voluntarily assume the discipline of either a lay practitioner who holds five precepts—to avoid killing, stealing, unwise sexual conduct, lying, and taking intoxicants—or of a monastic. Taking monastic precepts is not a requirement, but for those so inclined, it solidifies their intention and gives extra strength to their practice. The monastic precepts include basic ethical injunctions, such as to abandon killing, stealing, lying, and all sexual activity. They also include guidelines for living together as a community, for handling requisites for daily life such as food, clothing, shelter, and medicine, and for engaging with people within the monastic community, in the Buddhist community, and in the larger society in general. At the Buddha's time, the monastic order began as a loose group of wandering practitioners. Over time stable communities were formed, and such communities continue to this day. These communities enable monastics to study, practice, and observe together the precepts established by the Buddha.

As Buddhism spread to different areas in ancient India, several Vinaya schools arose. Of these, three are existent today: the Theravada, principally found in Sri Lanka and Southeast Asia; the Dharmagupta, chiefly followed in China, Vietnam, Korea, and Taiwan; and the Mulasarvastivada, mainly practiced among Tibetans. Although they have slightly different ways of enumerating the precepts, they are remarkably similar. All of these traditions set out various levels of ordination: novice (sramanera/sramanerika), probationary nun (*siksamana*), and full ordination (bhikshu/bhikshuni).

Each level of ordination has a corresponding number of precepts, and a candidate receives each ordination during a ceremony conducted by the sangha.

As a Buddhist monastic, one can live a variety of lifestyles; the only requisite is to observe the precepts as best one can. For example, a monastic may sometimes live in a monastery in the countryside and other times live in a flat in a city. She may have periods during which her life centers on service to the community and other periods when she focuses on study, teaching, or meditation. Sometimes she may live an active life amidst many people and other times do meditation retreat alone, observing silence for months. What remains constant in all these varying circumstances is that her day begins and ends with meditation and prayer, and during the day, she observes the monastic precepts as best she can. Such a variety of lifestyles is allowed, and a monastic adopts a particular one by following the guidance of her spiritual mentor.

Why would someone take monastic precepts? Undoubtedly there is a wide diversity of reasons according to each individual. Some of these reasons may be spiritual, others personal, and still others in response to society at a specific historical time and place. Following are some of the spiritual and practical reasons for taking monastic precepts that motivated me personally and are shared by a number of other monastics. Some of these reasons also apply to taking the lay precepts.

First, the precepts make us more aware of our actions. Living busy lives, we are often out of touch with ourselves and live "on automatic," going from one activity to another without much awareness of what we are doing or why. When we have precepts that guide and regulate our behavior, we want to follow them as purely as we can. To do this, we have to slow down, think before we speak or act, be aware of the thoughts and emotions that motivate us, and discern which produce happiness for self and others and which lead to suffering. For example, a person may rub her arm thoughtlessly whenever anything tickles it. After taking the precept to avoid killing living beings, including insects, she is more attentive and looks to see the cause of the tickling sensation before acting. Or, a person may sing TV commercial jingles and pop melodies mindlessly, either in her mind or out loud, totally unaware that she is doing so, and equally unaware that people around her may not want to hear them! After taking monastic precepts, she is more aware of what is going on in her mind and how it manifests outwardly as either speech or actions.

Precepts also help us to make clear ethical decisions. Each of us has ethical principles and lives according to them, but many of us re-negotiate them when it benefits our personal interest. For example, a person may believe that lying is harmful, and does not like when politicians, CEOs, or friends and relatives lie. However, from time to time when she does not want to have to deal with someone's reactions to what she did or does not want to admit to herself the ramifications of her actions, her mind rationalizes that "for the benefit of others," she needs to tell "a little white lie." This behavior clearly comes from personal, self-centered concerns, but at the time it seems not only logical but also proper. When she realizes the discrepancy between what she believes and how she acts, she asks herself, "Do I want to go through life like this? Do I want to continue being a hypocrite?" and sees that living according to precepts will help her to stop this self-centered and self-defeating behavior.

Seen in this way, precepts are not restricting, but liberating. They free us from doing things that in our hearts we do not want to do. Some people think, "Monastics can't do this and they can't do that. How do they have any fun in life? It must be horribly repressive to live like that." Someone with this view clearly should not become a monastic, for he or she will feel limited and constricted by the precepts. However, for someone who is happy as a monastic, the experience is very different. Having thought over the actions mentioned in the precepts and the karmic results of such activities in future lives, she wishes to abandon them. Nevertheless, because her attachment, anger, and ignorance are sometimes stronger than her wisdom, she finds herself involved in the very actions that she doesn't want to do. For example, she may wish to stop drinking or using recreational drugs, but when she is at a party with friends who use these substances, she thinks, "I want to fit in with everyone else. I'll feel out of place and others may think I'm strange if I don't join in. There's nothing bad about drinking. Anyway, I'll only take a little." Thus, her previous determination gets waylaid, and her old habits strongly arise again. However, when she has considered such situations in advance and made a strong determination not to follow her old habits, taking a precept regarding this behavior is a confirmation of her determination. Then, when she finds herself in such a situation, her mind does not get confused with doubts about what to do. Before taking the precept she has already decided. The precept has freed her from her detrimental habit and enabled her to act in the way that she wants to.

Taking ordination is a reflection of our inner decision to make our spiritual practice the center of our life. Most people have some spiritual interest and affinity, but the role these take is different in a monastic's life. While family life can be a useful ambience for spiritual practice, it also brings many distractions. As a monastic, we live simply. We do not have a family, a job, a mortgage to pay off, social engagements to fulfill, or children to put through college. We do not have the latest entertainment options in our residence. This leaves more time available for spiritual practice and teaching the Dharma. In addition, because we shave our hair, wear monastic robes, and do not use jewelry or cosmetics, we do not need to spend time buying a variety of clothes, deciding what to wear, or worrying about how we look.

Observing precepts—be they those of a monastic or those of a lay person—also enables us to approach liberation and enlightenment through purifying negative karma and accumulating positive potential. When we act destructively, we lay imprints in our mindstream that influence what we experience in the future; since the action is harmful, the result will be unpleasant. By abandoning our destructive behavior, we avoid creating negative karma that obscures our mindstream, and we purify the habitual energy that could make us act in that way again. In addition, since we are consciously abandoning harmful actions, we create positive potential that will bring happy results in the future and will make our mindstream more pliable and receptive to generating the realizations of the path to enlightenment. By observing precepts over time, we begin to feel a base of good energy and confidence, and this inner circumstance enables us to transform our mind readily and easily.

The Buddha's teachings are categorized into the Three Higher Trainings: the higher trainings in ethical discipline, meditative stabilization, and wisdom. Wisdom frees us from cyclic existence, and to develop and utilize it in that capacity, we need to have stable meditative concentration. Ethical discipline is the foundation for meditative stabilization and wisdom, for it acts as a tool to calm the grossest distractions and negative motivations in our mind. It is the easiest of the three higher trainings to complete, and observing precepts is a strong support in doing this.

The Buddha himself was a monastic, and this has great meaning. Living ethically, as demonstrated by keeping precepts, is the natural reflection of an enlightened mind. Although we are not yet enlightened, by keeping the precepts we attempt to emulate the Buddha's mental, verbal, and physical behavior.

Of course the question arises, "What happens if one breaks a precept?" The monastic precepts fall into various categories. To remain a monastic, we must avoid a complete transgression of any of the precepts in the first category, called defeat or *parajika*. These precepts forbid killing a human being, stealing something of value in the society, lying about our spiritual attainments, and sexual activity. The precepts in the other categories pertain to actions that are less severe but are easier to do. Before we are ordained, it is understood that we will most likely break some of the latter precepts. Why? Because our mind is not yet subdued. If we were able to keep the precepts perfectly, we would not need to take them. The precepts are tools to help us train our mind, speech, and behavior. The Buddha delineated the means by which we can purify and restore our precepts when we create an infraction: generating regret, making a determination to avoid the harmful action in the future, taking refuge in the Three Jewels, generating an altruistic intention, and engaging in some sort of remedial behavior. In the case of monastic precepts, the sangha meets together biweekly to do *posadha* (Pali: *uposatha*, Tibetan: *sojong*), the confession ceremony for purifying and restoring monastic precepts.

When the sangha community first came into being and for several years thereafter, no precepts existed. However, when some monastics began to act inappropriately, the Buddha established the precepts one by one in response to particular events. Some actions he prohibited, such as killing, are naturally negative or harmful no matter who does them. Other actions, for example watching entertainment, he proscribed for particular reasons. Although these actions are not negative in themselves, the Buddha prohibited them to avoid inconvenience to lay followers or to prevent distraction and loss of mindfulness by the monastics. For example, although taking intoxicants is not a naturally negative action, it is proscribed because a person who becomes intoxicated can more easily act in ways that directly harm himself or others.

The precepts were established in Indian society over twenty-five hundred years ago. Although times have changed, the basic functioning of the human mind has remained the same. Ignorance, anger, and attachment and the actions motivated by them are still the cause of our constantly recurring problems in cyclic existence. The Four Noble Truths, which describe our present situation and show us the way to transform it and liberate ourselves from suffering, are as true now as they were when the Buddha first taught them. Thus the basic thrust and design of monastic precepts hold true for the Western monastic of the twentieth and twenty-first centuries.

However, specific details in the precepts are more related to Indian society of the sixth century B.C. than to the modern West. For example, one of the bhikshuni precepts is to avoid riding in vehicles. In ancient India, vehicles were pulled by other people or by animals; thus riding in one could cause suffering to others. In addition, vehicles were used only by the wealthy and one could easily become arrogant by riding in one. However, in the West nowadays, neither of these concerns holds true. In fact, not riding in vehicles could be detrimental for others, for how else could a monastic go to a Dharma center to teach outside of his or her immediate locale?

Thus Western monastics must determine how to keep some of the precepts according to the society and situation in which they find themselves. When Buddhism spread from India to Tibet, China, and other countries, the way of keeping the precepts was also adjusted to fit the mentality of the society as well as the geography, climate, economics, and so on of the country. This process is only beginning in the West now. To facilitate it, we need to study the Buddha's teachings and the commentaries on them, as well as learn how other societies dealt with these challenges. Most of the talks in this book deal directly or indirectly with this theme.

THE ROLE OF MONASTICS
AND THE CONTRIBUTIONS OF THE NUNS

Living in the twentieth and twenty-first centuries we have inherited the benefit of work done by those before us. In particular, our hearts can open in gratitude for the Buddhist practitioners of previous generations, through whose kindness the teachings have been preserved in a pure form for us to enjoy today. The existence of the Buddhadharma and of the lineage of practitioners is dependent upon many people, monastic and lay alike. The entire Buddhist community of the past is responsible for the benefits we receive today.

Within that, monastics have traditionally played a special role in Buddhist societies. As people who leave the family life, their time is devoted predominantly to Dharma study, practice, and teachings, as well as to physically maintaining the monasteries, hermitages, and communities in which they live. Although there are many past and present highly realized lay practitioners, the main responsibility for the practice and preservation of the teachings has historically rested with monastics. For this reason, the monastic tradition has served a vital role in previous generations and needs to be preserved in our modern societies, East and West. It is not a life style suited to or desired by everyone, but it benefits those whom it suits, and they in turn benefit the larger society.

Since the Buddha's time, nuns have played an important, if largely unnoticed, role in keeping the Dharma alive. The *Therigatha,* or *Songs of the Elder Nuns,* was spoken by nuns who studied and practiced directly under the guidance of Shakyamuni Buddha. In it, they reveal their spiritual longing and achievements. Throughout the centuries and in all Buddhist societies, nuns have studied, practiced, and in many cases taught the Dharma. Due to the structure of society and the nuns' reticence to draw attention to themselves, many of their contributions have gone unnoticed.

At present we see active and vibrant Buddhist nuns in the East and the West as well. Some are scholars, others meditators. Some work on translations of scriptures, others do social service work in hospitals, prisons, and schools in war zones or in poor areas. As the talks in this book reveal, the contribution of these nuns is a wonderful work in progress.

HISTORY AND MONASTIC DISCIPLINE

HISTORY OF BUDDHIST MONASTICISM
AND ITS WESTERN ADAPTATION

Bhikshuni Karma Lekshe Tsomo

Melissa Vincenty

B̲hikshuni Karma Lekshe Tsomo grew up in Hawaii and received her M.A. in Asian Studies from the University of Hawaii in 1971. She studied for five years at the Library of Tibetan Works and Archives and several years at the Institute of Buddhist Dialectics, both in Dharamsala, India. In 1977, she received sramanerika ordination and in 1982 bhikshuni ordination. She is a founding member of Sakyadhita, the founder of Jamyang Choling Nunnery in Dharamsala, and is currently completing her Ph.D. at the University of Hawaii.

A THOROUGH DISCUSSION OF THE TRANSMISSION OF BUDDHIST MONASTICISM AND ITS ADAPTATION IN WESTERN CULTURES WOULD TAKE VOLUMES. Moreover, this historical process is still in its initial stages and is so multifaceted that any conclusions drawn at this point would be premature. Here I shall simply explore a few of the issues involved. Some of the points I raise may be controversial, but both critical and comparative analyses are essential to an understanding of the momentous meeting of cultures presently underway. Moreover, the spirit of free inquiry is wholly compatible with Buddhist thinking.

The sangha, the order of Buddhist renunciants, began near Varanasi with five young men from respected Brahmin families who became monks not long after the Buddha achieved enlightenment and started teaching. Gradually they were joined by thousands of other bhikshus (fully ordained monks) and a few years later by hundreds of bhikshunis (fully ordained nuns) as well. The early sangha was disproportionately upper caste, with its members from the better-educated classes of Indian society.

The Buddhist order was not the first in India. Jain and Brahmanical communities, which served as prototypes for the early sangha, were already established. Surviving documents revealing how daily life was regulated in these communities offer evidence that the early Buddhist mendicants adopted some organizational features from them. For example, followers of contemporary religious groups gathered together periodically, so the early sangha also began to gather on new moon and full moon days. At first they sat silently, but followers of other sects criticized them for sitting "like dumb pigs," so the Buddha instructed them to read the *Pratimoksa Sutra* containing their precepts on these occasions. This tradition of the bhikshu sangha reciting the *Bhikshu Pratimoksa Sutra* and the bhikshuni sangha reciting the *Bhikshuni Pratimoksa Sutra* is one of the three essential rites of the monastic community. The other two are the rite commencing the rainy season retreat (*varsa*) and the rite concluding it (*pravarana*). Other rites developed to help regulate the life of the sangha, including precise instructions for conducting ordinations and methods for resolving disputes.[1]

In the beginning the bhikshus lived an itinerant lifestyle, staying at the foot of trees and going to villages and towns to gather their daily meal in an alms bowl and to give Dharma teachings. Although they were dependent upon the lay followers for alms, the optimal condition for achieving liberation was said to be staying in seclusion in the forest, aloof from society. As the sangha grew, the Buddha sent the bhikshus out to disseminate the teachings far and wide saying, "Let not two go in the same direction." This instruction helped prevent the formation of strong bonds of attachment to places or people. Gradually the bhikshus and bhikshunis began to assemble in seasonal settlements (*vihara*) for three months during the rainy season to avoid stepping on the insects that abounded during that time. Eventually these *viharas* became more or less fixed residences, developing into separate communities for the bhikshus and bhikshunis. These single-sex communities included sramaneras (male novices) and sramanerikas (female novices), who were training to receive the full precepts. The Buddhists may have been the first renunciants in India to establish organized monastic communities, many of which evolved into educational centers.[2] Relieved of household responsibilities and attachments, the monks and nuns were able to concentrate single-pointedly on living a disciplined life and achieving the goal of liberation.

THE PURPOSE AND PRACTICE OF THE PRECEPTS

The Sanskrit word for becoming a Buddhist renunciant is *pabbajiya* meaning "going forth." It signifies leaving the household life and entering a state of homelessness. After becoming a renunciant, a person is expected to train for ten years (or at least a minimum of five) under the close guidance of a qualified senior bhikshu or bhikshuni preceptor.[3] After some years of such training, one might enter the second stage of ordination, receiving the *upasampada* or ordination as a bhikshu or bhikshuni, signifying full admission into the sangha, or monastic order.

The Vinaya, the corpus of advice and incidents related to monastic discipline, was not originally formulated as a separate body of texts, but was an integral part of the Dharma teachings. When the order began, no set code of regulations for Buddhist mendicants existed. The regulations, or precepts, were established as needed beginning with the rule of *brahmacarya* ("pure conduct," meaning celibacy) after one of the early monks returned home and slept with his wife.[4] Gradually over two hundred precepts were formulated on the basis of the misconduct of the bhikshus and about one hundred more on that of the bhikshunis.[5]

That the bhikshunis have roughly one hundred precepts more than the bhikshus has been interpreted by some as evidence that women have more delusions than men and by some as evidence of sexism in Buddhism. Examined historically, however, neither interpretation is justified. Instead, it appears that as the bhikshuni sangha evolved, the nuns inherited most of the precepts formulated for the bhikshu sangha, and additional precepts were formulated as incidents arose involving nuns, particularly a nun named Thullananda and her followers. Some of these latter precepts, such as the ones prohibiting nuns from travelling alone, clearly are designed to protect them from danger and exploitation. Other precepts, such as the one requiring bhikshunis to receive instructions from a bhikshu twice a month (but not vice versa), clearly reflect gender inequalities in Indian society at that time.

The Pratimoksa texts contain the specific injunctions by which Buddhist monks and nuns live, the precepts that help them regulate their lives.[6] These injunctions are an integral part of Buddhist ethics as a whole, helping practitioners create a conducive environment, physical and psychological, for spiritual practice. They help them, for example, to ensure the smooth functioning of the Buddhist monastic community and to protect the sangha from the criticism of the lay community. The Vinaya texts establish a baseline for acceptable conduct for Buddhist monastics and provide a framework within which sangha members may make informed judgments on how best to conduct their lives and nurture their practice of virtue.

The purpose of the Buddhist monastic code is to establish optimal conditions for the achievement of liberation. Observing the precepts helps beings control the passions that entangle them in samsara and fosters the awareness needed to precipitate liberation. Many times in the texts the Buddha says, "Come, o monk, live the *brahmacarya* life in order that you may put an end to suffering." The Pratimoksa texts emphasize the practice of virtuous actions and the forswearing of negative actions in order to progress toward liberation from cyclic existence.

Sangha members make a voluntary, usually lifelong, commitment to maintain certain precepts and standards of behavior; it is important to consider this commitment seriously before making it. The most fundamental requirements are to refrain from sexual conduct; taking life; taking what is not given; telling untruths; taking intoxicants; attending entertainment; using ornaments, cosmetics, and perfumes; sitting on luxurious seats and beds; taking food at unregulated times; and handling silver and gold. In addition, many other precepts help monastics remain mindful of every action in daily life. To take the precepts lightly, saying "This precept is not that important," or "This precept is impossible to keep," violates the precept that prohibits belittling the precepts. To the casual observer, many of the secondary precepts appear trivial and irrelevant to spiritual pursuit; even to the dedicated practitioner their abundance can be discouraging. Harkening back to the classic clerical debate over the letter versus the spirit of the rule, one may also argue that adhering to technical correctness rather than embodying the spirit of the precepts is counterproductive to the achievement of liberation.

Of course, it is difficult to keep all the precepts purely. Differences in social conditions now and at the time of the Buddha require thoughtful adaptation of the precepts in the present day. Making wise decisions in adapting the precepts requires a thorough study of the precedents, described in the Vinaya texts, upon which the precepts were formulated.[7] In addition, years of training under careful guidance are required to learn how to appropriately handle everyday situations, especially in the West. Monastics often fall short of their own expectations and occasionally commit infractions of the precepts—walking on the grass, handling silver or gold, digging the ground, and so on—but a clear understanding of the Vinaya injunctions provides criteria for making decisions and serves as a foundation for building a solid practice.

The patched robes and shaved head, the most obvious signs of a Buddhist's monastic commitment, may be inconvenient sometimes, evoking mixed reactions of curiosity, admiration, or disdain from friends and passersby, but they are also a powerful incentive for mindful awareness. Wearing robes entails an obligation of honesty with regard to one's moral conduct: it is a declaration that one is observing the precepts of a Buddhist monastic, so to wear them without keeping the precepts is dishonest. Sangha members are traditionally regarded as worthy of trust, respect, and offerings. To acquire these benefits undeservedly by misrepresenting oneself is a serious matter. The dangers implicit in according all members of the Buddhist community the status of sangha, whether they are abiding by precepts or not, should be abundantly clear. These days many Westerners commonly refer to all members of Dharma centers as sangha, although this is not the traditional usage of the term. Although it is possible for lay people to be exemplars of ethical conduct, those who have made a commitment to strict monastic discipline have traditionally been regarded a field of merit.

Although the monastic code can and needs to be interpreted within the context of culture, place, and time, the Vinaya texts are part of the Buddhist canon and cannot simply be revised at will. The various Buddhist monastic cultures observed in the world today—Chinese, Japanese, Thai, Tibetan, and so on—are the results of a synthesis of Vinaya and the local norms and customs of the countries where Buddhism spread. One of the most striking features of the world's various Buddhist cultures is the common legacy of monastic discipline—the robes, the mores, the spiritual ideals—that each of these preserves in its own unique way.

As we may recall, it was the sight of a renunciant who appeared peaceful and contented that inspired Buddha Shakyamuni's renunciation of worldly life. The image of this renunciant made a striking impression on the young prince, who had been shocked by his recent encounters with sickness, old age, and death, and his resultant realization that these sufferings are intrinsic to the human condition. To inspire others to develop renunciation and take up the spiritual path, then, is one of the roles that a monastic plays. This is a huge responsibility.

Nuns and monks cannot become genuine models of simplicity and contentment unless we live simple and contented lives. If we are caught up in consumerism, greed, and attachment—wanting more comfort, more possessions, better possessions—then we are spinning on the wheel of desire like everyone else and do not represent an alternative lifestyle for others. It comes down to this question: If nuns and monks live, act, and talk like worldly people, are we really fulfilling the socially beneficial role that is expected of a monastic? In an age when the clergy of various religions in many countries are coming under scrutiny for lavish indulgences and moral transgressions, Western nuns and monks have the opportunity to help revitalize Buddhism by reaffirming the original purity and simplicity of spiritual life.

Paradoxes in Monastic Life

In the beginning the Buddha exhorted the bhikshus and bhikshunis to "wander solitary as a rhinoceros." As time went on and the number of nuns and monks grew, the Buddhist sangha was criticized for roaming around and trampling crops, so gradually many gave up their eremitic lifestyle and settled in cenobitic communities. In a sense, then, Buddhist monasticism represents a rejection of social expectations yet, whether as mendicants or settled contemplatives, nuns and monks are trained to be very conscious of social expectations. The apparent tension here reveals the push and shove in monastic life between self-oriented personal practice and other-oriented community life—the contrast between liberation from the constraints of the world on one hand, and concern for community and society on the other. It mirrors a larger dichotomy between the mystical ideal of the absolutely unconditioned and the mundane, reflected in the strict observance of precise, practical rules. Such contrasts illustrate the paradoxes implicit in Buddhist monastic life.

On a personal level, a tension exists between the desire for solitude and the desire to be of immediate service to living beings "in the world." Perhaps influenced by their Judeo-Christian cultural background, most Western monastics become ordained with the intention, at least in part, of helping people and contributing to the betterment of society. Because Buddhism is new to the West, many opportunities arise for social service—establishing centers, teaching, leading retreats, serving teachers, translating, counseling newcomers, running a Buddhist center, and responding to requests from the wider community. However, these activities—important as they are—clearly leave little time for personal practice. We begin to feel guilty taking time away from the multifaceted needs of the Buddhist community for individual study and meditation. Yet, without a strong personal practice, we lack the inner resources to adequately serve the community's needs. Ironically, developing the inner spiritual qualities needed to benefit sentient beings requires thorough study and reflection, which requires periodic withdrawal from the very beings we wish to serve.

Another paradox in monastic life concerns the range of images and expectations that a nun or monk confronts when living in the West. The lay community has high expectations of monastics and sometimes expects them to be saints. On the other hand they want them to be "human," with all the human frailties, so that they can "identify with them." Unrealistic expectations of saintliness can make monastics feel totally inadequate to their chosen task, often pushing them beyond their physical and emotional limitations; whereas the expectation that they exhibit human frailties can cause lapses in discipline. Monastics are expected to be at once reclusive—masters of meditation and ritual—and social—responding selflessly to the emotional and psychological needs of all who petition them. These contrasting expectations ignore the fact that individuals come to monastic life with a range of personalities, inclinations, and capabilities. For each one to be all things to all people is impossible, however hard we may try. This creates an inner tension between what we expect ourselves to embody spiritually and what we realistically could have achieved at this point, as beginners on the path. Trying to use this tension between spiritual ideals and psychological realities creatively, for spiritual progress, is one of the greatest challenges for a practitioner, lay or ordained. The process of skillfully negotiating the ideal and the ordinary, pride and discouragement, discipline and repose, requires a raw personal honesty that only relentless spiritual practice can engender.

Another paradox concerns the material well-being of Western nuns and monks. The original mendicant lifestyle practiced in India is difficult to replicate in contemporary Western countries. Although ethnic Buddhist communities generally care for the material needs of monastics in the temples of their particular traditions, Western monastics find few places outside Asia where they can live a monastic lifestyle. Thus, Western nuns and monks are often monastics without a monastery. Nuns and monks living at Gampo Abbey in Nova Scotia and Amaravati in England are the exceptions. Other ordained Western Buddhists find that issues of livelihood—food, shelter, and medical expenses, for example—require a great deal of energy that could otherwise be directed to spiritual practice.

The general public, including Western Buddhists themselves, often assumes that Buddhist monastics are cared for by an order, as are Christian monastics, and are surprised to learn that newly-ordained Western nuns and monks may be left to deal with issues of sustenance completely on their own. They may serve without compensation as teachers, translators, secretaries, cooks, and psychological counselors in the Dharma center and also work at an outside job in order to pay for their own rent, food, and personal expenses. They are expected to play the role of a monastic and do much more, without the benefits traditionally accorded a monastic.

The wide spectrum of choices that Western monastics make concerning issues of livelihood was evident at the 1996 Bodhgaya training course, *Life as a Western Buddhist Nun*. At one end of the spectrum were two nuns from Amaravati who had not touched money for sixteen years; at the other end was a nun who supported herself as a registered nurse, wore lay clothes and longish hair for her job, and had a mortgage on her apartment and taxes to pay. Because adequate monastic communities have yet to be developed, most ordained Westerners face the pressures of playing both the role of a monastic and that of an ordinary citizen. They must deal with the incongruity between the ideal mendicant lifestyle from the time of the Buddha and the modern ideal of economic self-sufficiency. Resolving the paradox between the ideal of renunciation and the realities of survival is one of the great challenges faced by Western Buddhist monastics.

CREATING MONASTIC COMMUNITIES FOR WOMEN

At the time of the Buddha nuns received their "going forth" (*pabbajiya*) and training under the guidance of nuns. Although monks in the early days were assumed to have greater knowledge and authority, nuns felt more comfortable discussing personal matters with nuns, rather than monks, and were able to receive closer personal guidance by training under them. Even though bhikshus confirm bhikshuni ordinations, as stipulated in the Vinaya texts, the tradition of nuns receiving ordination and training from nuns has continued in many monasteries until today, particularly in China and Korea.

In countries such as Thailand, Sri Lanka, and Tibet, however, the ordination of nuns has been conducted almost exclusively by bhikshus. In a way, this makes sense, since these bhikshu precept masters are well respected and experienced in performing these ceremonies. On the other hand, it means that monks have the power to decide who joins the nuns' order without consulting the nuns. This creates a problem. The bhikshus ordain women, but they often do not provide them with food, accommodations, or training. Previously ordained nuns have no choice but to accept these novices, even if they are not at all suited to monastic life. Monasteries for nuns must figure out some way to feed and house the newcomers or are put in the awkward position of having to refuse them admission to their monasteries. There have also been cases where bhikshus have ordained women who are physically unwell, psychologically or emotionally unstable, or mentally disabled. Although it is contrary to the Vinaya to ordain unfit people, once they are ordained, the situation becomes very difficult. Senior nuns and their monasteries are liable to be criticized if they are not able to care for these new nuns.

Now I would like to bluntly raise the issue of women's reliance on men and recommend that women develop monastic communities independently. Of course nuns are deeply indebted and deeply grateful for all the support, encouragement, and teachings we have received from excellent male teachers and I am not suggesting that we sever or diminish these important relationships in any way. Instead, I am suggesting that women, and nuns in particular, need to assume, with wisdom and skillful means, a greater sense of responsibility for our own future. We need to address straightforwardly issues of autonomy and leadership, cutting dependencies on male authority, instilling a sense of self-reliance, and fostering independent communities.

Many women both in Asian and Western societies are male-identified. This is natural in patriarchal societies, where men are valued over women. Male-identified women respect men, ask and accept advice from men, work for men, support men materially, look to men for approval, and provide men with food, lodging, all necessities, and often luxuries, even when they do not have enough themselves. This is not a new phenomenon. During the Buddha's time an elderly nun was found to have passed out from lack of food, because she had given the food in her alms bowl to a monk. When the Buddha heard about this, he prohibited monks from accepting alms that had been collected by nuns.

It is important to question honestly whether the tendency to identify with males is appropriate for nuns. In leaving household life, nuns reject the traditional role of subordination to a husband or male partner. We renounce the role of a sex object available for men's enjoyment and enter a community of women where we can be free of men's authority. Therefore, it seems a bit strange if nuns, having achieved a state of freedom and independence, then choose to rely constantly on men. Men have their own concerns and responsibilities. No matter how compassionate they are, monks cannot be expected to take full responsibility for nuns' communities. Nuns need to develop self-reliance and self-confidence and begin to take full responsibility for their own communities. At present, due to a scarcity of qualified female teachers, that is, Tripitaka masters, nuns have no choice but to rely on male teachers in developing study programs. But I suggest that women adopt the goal of nurturing and developing themselves as fully qualified teachers and spiritual masters capable of guiding not only other women, but society at large.

Excellent models of autonomous monastic communities for women exist today in Taiwan and Korea. In the past few years these communities have inspired education and meditation training programs for women in locations as widespread as Sri Lanka, Thailand, and the Indian Himalayas. Autonomous monastic communities for men have been a staple of Asian life for centuries. Now, with the acculturation of Buddhism in the West, we have the opportunity to focus attention on developing autonomous monastic communities for women that are equally valued. Buddhist women teachers in both Asia and the West are demonstrating that spiritual leadership is not only a possibility for women, but is already an everyday reality.

NOTES:
1 An extensive discussion of the procedures used for resolving disputes is found in Sunanda Putuwar's *The Buddhist Sangha: Paradigm of the Ideal Human Society* (Lanham, MD: University Press of American, 1991), p.69-90.
2 A detailed examination of sangha organization is found Ibid., p. 34-46.
3 For a description of this training, see Nand Kishore Prasad, *Studies in Buddhist and Jaina Monachism* (Vaishali, Bihar: Research Institute of Prakrit, Jainology and Ahimsa, 1972), p. 94-99.
4 The history and complexity of the term *brahmacarya* are discussed in Jotiya Dhirasekeraa's *Buddhist Monastic Discipline: A Study of its Origin and Development* (Colombo: Ministry of Higher Education, 1982), p. 21-32.
5 For the precepts of the bhikshus, including extensive commentary, see Thanissaro

Bhikkhu (Geoffrey DeGraff), *The Buddhist Monastic Code* (Metta Forest Monastery, P.O. Box 1409, Valley Center, CA 92082, 1994), and Charles S. Prebish, *Buddhist Monastic Discipline: The Sanskrit Pratimoka Sutras of the Mahasamghikas and Mulasarvastivadins* (University Park and London: Pennsylvania State University Press, 1975). For the precepts of the bhikshunis, see Karma Lekshe Tsomo, *Sisters in Solitude: Two Traditions of Buddhist Monastic Precepts for Women* (Albany, NY: State University of New York Press, 1996).

6 For a discussion of the etymology of the term Pratimoksa, see Sukumar Dutt, *Early Monachism* (New Delhi: Munshiram Manoharlal Publishers, 1984), p. 71-75.

7 Additional commentary on the precepts is found in the Somdet Phra Maha Samaa Chao Krom Phraya, *Samantapasadika: Buddhaghosa's Commentary on the Vinaya Pitaka*, Vol. 8 (London: Pali Text Society, 1977).

THE HISTORY OF THE BHIKKHUNI SANGHA

Dr. Chatsumarn Kabilsingh

Born in Thailand in 1944, Dr. Chatsumarn Kabilsingh graduated with Honors in Philosophy from Visva Bharati University (India), received her M.A. degree in Religion from McMaster University (Canada), and her Ph.D. from Magadh University (India) in 1982. Since 1973, she has been an Associate Professor of Philosophy and Religion and is now head of the Department of Philosophy and Religion at Thammasat University, Bangkok. She has published several books and many research articles, attends international conferences, is the editor of Yasodhara, *and is past president of Sakyadhita, an international organization of Buddhist women.*

THE BHIKKHUNI ORDER WAS ESTABLISHED AT THE TIME OF THE BUDDHA AND EXISTS UNTIL THIS DAY. For centuries, ordained women have practiced, realized, and upheld the Buddha's teachings, benefiting not only themselves but also the societies in which they lived. Here I will give a brief history of the order, including its spread to other countries, and discuss interesting points in the Vinaya.

When King Suddhodana, the Buddha's father, passed away, his stepmother and aunt, Mahapajapati, together with five hundred royal women, went to the Buddha who was in Kapilavatthu to request permission to join the sangha. The Buddha responded, "Do not ask so." She repeated the request again three times, and each time the Buddha simply said, "Do not ask so." Nobody knew what he was thinking, and it is not clear why he refused. However, that the Buddha hesitated to accept her into the sangha has been interpreted by some to mean that the Buddha did not want women to join the order. Therefore, some people think that it was no problem when the bhikkhuni order died out in India approximately one thousand years later. In our study of the historical development of the bhikkhuni sangha, when others quote from the texts to prove authoritatively that the bhikkhuni order cannot be restored today, we have to be equally conversant and fluent in quoting from the texts to prove that it can.

The Buddha left Kapilavatthu and went to Vesali, which was many days' journey on foot. By that time, Mahapajapati had shaved her head and put on the robes. Together with five hundred royal women who had done the same, she walked to Vesali, thus demonstrating women's determination to be ordained and follow the Buddha. Once there, she sat by the entrance to the *vihara*, weeping, her feet swollen and bleeding from the journey. Ananda, the Buddha's cousin and attendant, saw the women, spoke with them and learned of their problem. He approached the Buddha on their behalf saying, "Mahapajapati, your aunt and stepmother, is here, waiting for you to give her permission to join the order." Again, the Buddha said, "Do not ask so." Ananda tried another tact, "After all, your aunt is also your stepmother. She was the one who fed you with her milk." The Buddha still refused. Then Ananda asked, "Are you not giving permission because women do not have the same spiritual potential as men to become enlightened?" The Buddha said, "No, Ananda, women are equal to men in their potential to achieve enlightenment." This statement opened a new horizon in the world of religion in general at that time. Previously, no founder of any religion had proclaimed men and women to have equal potential for enlightenment.

Then, the Buddha said he would give women permission to join the order if Mahapajapati would accept the eight *gurudhamma*—eight important rules—as the nuns' garland to decorate themselves. Mahapajapati did. One of these rules is very annoying to many Western Buddhist scholars; it says that a nun ordained even a hundred years must bow to a monk ordained but one day. By Western standards, it seems as if nuns are being suppressed, but there is another way to look at this. The Vinaya recounts the story of six monks who lifted up their robes to show their thighs to the nuns. When the Buddha learned about this, he made an exception to that rule and told the nuns not to pay respect to these monks. A nun, then, does not have to bow to every monk, but only to a monk who is worthy of respect. We need to understand each *gurudhamma* properly, for the Buddha always made exceptions after the general rule was established.

One of the *gurudhamma* mentions *sikkhamanas*, probationary nuns who train for two years in preparation to become bhikkhunis. It says that after a probationary nun has trained with a bhikkhuni for two years, that bhikkhuni preceptor has the responsibility to fully ordain her. However, when the Buddha ordained Mahapajapati, there were no probationary nuns. He ordained her directly as a bhikkhuni. So how do we explain that within the eight important rules, one of them states that before becoming a bhikkhuni, a woman must be a probationary nun? In addressing this, an English monk told me he believes that the *gurudhamma* arose much later on, and were shifted to the forefront by the monks who were the historical recorders. These eight important rules very clearly put nuns in a position subordinate to monks, so it would have been to the monks' advantage for the recorders to attribute them to the Buddha.

The Buddha may have hesitated to accept women into the order for several reasons. One might have been his compassion for the nuns, especially his aunt, for the bhikkhus and bhikkhunis received their food by collecting alms in the villages. Sometimes they received very little, just a handful of rice, a piece of bread, or some kind of vegetables. Imagine the elderly queen Mahapajapati and five hundred royal women going out begging. It would have been almost impossible because they had led such comfortable lives in the palace. Maybe out of compassion the Buddha did not want these women to face such hardship.

In addition, at that time there were no monasteries. The monastics lived a very difficult lifestyle, dwelling under trees and in caves. Who would give this group of wandering women dwelling places? Moreover, who would teach the nuns? They could be ordained, shave their heads, and put on robes, but if they did not receive an education and training, they would be just like any wanderer in India at that time. No plan for educating them existed yet. Later, it was established that the bhikkhu sangha could assign a few excellent monks to teach the nuns.

Furthermore, the Buddha had already received criticism from lay people that he was destroying the family unit. To accept five hundred women into the order implied that he was going to destroy five hundred families because women were the heart of the family. However, later the Buddha learned that the husbands of these women had already joined the order. Thus by ordaining the women, he would not break up those families. The Buddha must have thought through all these issues, and upon realizing that the problems could be overcome, he accepted the nuns into the order.

It is also possible that he had never thought about women joining the order prior to Mahapajapati's request because in ancient India, women never left household life. In fact, it was unthinkable for women to be on their own at that time. Even nowadays in India, women seldom leave the family. But since the Buddha knew that enlightenment was a possibility for all human beings, he opened the door for women to be ordained. This was a revolutionary step given the social climate at the time.

Thus the bhikkhuni sangha was formed about seven or eight years after the bhikkhu sangha. I see this as one of the reasons the Buddha made the bhikkhuni sangha subordinate to the bhikkhu sangha. They are subordinate in the sense of being younger sisters and elder brothers, not in the sense of being masters and slaves.

It was recorded that just after admitting women into the sangha, the Buddha said, "Because I have accepted women into the order, Buddhadhamma will only last five hundred years." I view this statement as a reflection of the mentality of the monks who first recorded the Vinaya in written form in Sri Lanka 400-450 years after the Buddha's *parinibbana*. These monks apparently did not agree that women should join the order. Some Western scholars think that this statement was later attributed to the Buddha but was not really his. As we see, over twenty-five hundred years have gone by, and not only is Buddhism still prospering in Asia but it is also spreading to the West. The prophecy saying that the Buddhadhamma would last only five hundred years because women joined the sangha is invalid.

Questioning the authenticity of certain passages in the Buddhist scriptures is a delicate issue, and we have to be very careful. How can we prove that everything was passed down exactly as the Buddha spoke it? On the other hand, isn't there danger in saying that certain passages are later interpolations? I become suspicious only when a passage does not correspond with the spirit of the main core of the Buddha's teachings. In general, we have to trust that the Indian monks had accurate memories and be grateful to them for preserving and transmitting the texts. The Buddhist monks were meticulous in preserving the teachings and handing them down. In Christianity, different men wrote the Four Gospels and they did not confer among themselves, while the Buddhist monastics held councils to compile and systematize the Buddha's teachings, during which they checked each other's information. The first council was held just after the Buddha's passing and five hundred arhats attended. The second one occurred one hundred years after that, with seven hundred monks coming together to recite the agreed upon body of knowledge.

THE RELATIONSHIP BETWEEN THE BHIKKHU AND THE BHIKKHUNI SANGHA

As we would expect, the monks treated the nuns in the same way that men in general treated women in Indian society at that time. When women joined the order, the monks expected them to clean the monastery and to wash their dishes, robes, and rugs. Lay people noticed this and reported it to the Buddha, saying that these women wanted to be ordained so that they could study and practice the teachings, but now they had little time for these. In response, the Buddha established rules for monks regarding how to treat nuns. For example, he established precepts forbidding monks to ask bhikkhunis to wash their robes, sitting cloths, and so on.

The Buddha also protected nuns from being taken advantage of by lax monks. One 120-year-old bhikkhuni went on almsround each morning, walking the long distance from the monastery to the village. She received food and took it back to the monastery in her almsbowl. At the entrance to the monastery waited a young monk, who was too lazy to walk into the village for alms. Noticing that his bowl was empty, she offered her food to him. It was enough for only one person, so she then had nothing to eat for the rest of the day.

The next day, he waited for her again, and again she offered him her food. On the third day, after having not eaten for three days, she went to the village to collect alms. A carriage owned by a wealthy supporter of Buddhism passed very near to her, and as she stepped out of its way, she fainted and fell to the ground. The rich man stopped to help her and discovered that she fainted because she had not eaten for three days. He reported the situation to the Buddha and protested that a nun had been treated that way by a monk. The Buddha thereby established the precept prohibiting monks from taking food from bhikkhunis. Of course, understanding the spirit of each precept is important; this one does not mean that nuns having plenty of food should not share it with monks.

Nuns at the time of the Buddha had equal rights and an equal share in everything. In one case, eight robes were offered to both sanghas at a place where there was only one nun and four monks. The Buddha divided the robes in half, giving four to the nun and four to the monks, because the robes were for both sanghas and had to be divided equally however many were in each group. Because the nuns tended to receive fewer invitations to lay people's homes, the Buddha had all offerings brought to the monastery and equally divided between the two sanghas. He protected the nuns and was fair to both parties.

The First Council and the Bhikkhuni Patimokkha

Ananda, the Buddha's attendant, played a very important role in relation to the nuns. He was well liked by the nuns and visited many nunneries in order to teach them. Because he heard almost all of the Buddha's teachings and had a phenomenal memory, he was a key person at the First Council when the teachings were recited and collected.

That some monks had not been happy that the Buddha allowed women to join the order had never been expressed while the Buddha was alive. It first came out at the First Council, which five hundred male arhats attended about three months after the Buddha's *parinibbana*, his passing away. Before the actual recitation of the Buddha's teachings, they told Ananda he had made eight mistakes and forced him to confess to these. One was that he had introduced women into the sangha. Ananda responded that he did not see that as a mistake, nor did he violate a precept in doing so. However, in order to avoid causing schism in the sangha so soon after the Buddha's *parinibbana*, he said that if the monks wanted him to confess, he would do so.

I have doubts that only men—five hundred male arhats—were at this council. On *uposatha* days every new and full moon, the bhikkhunis would recite their *Patimokkha Sutta* apart from the monks. I believe that technically, it could not be possible for the monks to recite the *Patimokkha Sutta* of the nuns, and so bhikkhunis must have been present at the First Council. The recorders, who were all monks, may not have thought it important to mention their presence. Some monks have been kind enough to speak about this point: recently, a Sri Lankan monk told me that he too did not think that only men attended the First Council.

THE BHIKKHUNI ORDER IN INDIA AND ITS SPREAD TO OTHER COUNTRIES

Both the bhikkhu and bhikkhuni sanghas existed until the eleventh century A.D. when the Muslims attacked India and wiped out the Buddhist monasteries. In 248 B.C.E., about three hundred years after the passing away of the Buddha, King Asoka the Great came to the throne. A great supporter of Buddhism, he sent Buddhist missionaries in nine different directions. His own son, Mahinda Thera, traveled to Sri Lanka to teach the Dhamma and establish the bhikkhu sangha. Princess Anula, the sister-in-law of King Devanampiyatissa of Sri Lanka, converted to Buddhism when he did. After listening to the teachings of Mahinda Thera, she became a stream-enterer and asked him if she could join the sangha. Mahinda Thera told her that dual ordination by both the bhikkhu and the bhikkhuni orders was necessary to become a bhikkhuni. At least five bhikkhunis must be present to form a sangha, and the preceptor must have at least twelve years standing as a bhikkhuni in order to give the precepts. He suggested that she ask King Devanampiyatissa to send a messenger to India to request King Asoka to send his daughter, Sanghamitta Theri, and some other bhikkhunis to give the ordination. Sanghamitta Theri, a princess, had given up royal luxury to practice the Dhamma. Well versed in the Vinaya, she also taught the Dhamma. Thus, upon request from the king of Sri Lanka, King Asoka sent Sanghamitta Theri and other bhikkhunis to establish the nuns' order in Sri Lanka. With her, King Asoka also sent a branch of the bodhi tree from Bodhgaya. She and the other Indian bhikkhunis, together with the bhikkhu sangha, ordained Princess Anula and other Sri Lankan women, thus establishing the bhikkhuni sangha in Sri Lanka, the first one outside India.

Hundreds of women wanted to receive ordination when Sanghamitta Theri arrived, and King Devanampiyatissa set about building nunneries for them. The bhikkhuni sangha prospered there along side the bhikkhu sangha, until both the orders were wiped out when the Chola King from Southern India attacked Sri Lanka in 1017 A.D. The next Buddhist king who came to the throne searched the entire island and found only one male novice left. To revive the sangha in Sri Lanka, he sent envoys to Burma and Thailand to request the kings there to send monastics to give ordination in Sri Lanka. However, since Thailand never had the bhikkhuni order, no bhikkhunis could be sent, and the Sri Lankan king was able to revive only the bhikkhu sangha.

The Chinese Nuns

From the second century A.D., Chinese men were ordained as monks. In the early fourth century, one Chinese woman, Ching-chien, was very enthusiastic to become a bhikkhuni. Although she received sramanerika ordination from a monk, she did not receive bhikkhuni ordination, because the Chinese monks said that dual ordination was necessary. Later, a foreign monk, T'an-mo-chieh, said that insisting women receive dual ordination was not practical in a land where no bhikkhunis were present. He and a bhikkhu sangha ordained Ching-chien, whereupon she became the first bhikkhuni in China.

Later the Chinese people invited bhikkhunis from Sri Lanka to come to China. Some came, though not enough to give the bhikkhuni ordination. These nuns remained in China to study the Chinese language, while the ship owner returned to Sri Lanka to invite enough bhikkhunis to come to China to give the ordination. The following year, the ship brought many bhikkhunis from Sri Lanka, including one named Tessara. Together with the Sri Lankan bhikkhunis who had arrived earlier, they gave ordination to more than three hundred Chinese women at Southern Grove Monastery. The Indian monk Sanghavarman and the bhikkhu sangha also gave the ordination, making this the first dual ordination of bhikkhunis in China.

According to the Theravada Vinaya found in Southeast Asia—and this is different from the Dharmagupta Vinaya found in China—a bhikkhuni preceptor can give ordination to only one nun every alternate year. Nowadays some people question the validity of the Chinese ordination because many nuns are ordained together. However, when we study the spirit of the precept, it is evident why initially the number of disciples each bhikkhuni preceptor ordained was limited. First, for safety reasons, the nuns could not live in the forest, but had to stay in dwellings, and there weren't enough of these.

Secondly, the number of Indian women ordaining was so great that the bhikkhuni sangha did not have enough teachers to train them. One way of limiting the population of nuns was to limit the number of women each preceptor could ordain. In China, the situation was different, and it was practical to ordain many bhikkhunis at once.

Earlier this century, many huge monasteries existed in Mainland China. Before the communist takeover, the monks thought they were strong and would be able to survive. However, when the nuns heard that China might be taken over by the communists, they started to migrate to Taiwan. They brought their resources along with them, began to build nunneries, and became well settled in Taiwan. When the communists took over the mainland, the monks realized that they could not survive under the communist rule, so they fled to Taiwan in a hurry and arrived with almost nothing. The nuns' sangha gave them considerable help as they became reestablished. The monks remember their kindness, and thus the nuns in Taiwan are well respected by both the monks and the lay Buddhists. The nuns far outnumber the monks, are well educated, and have strong communities with their own abbesses.

Taiwan is a stronghold for bhikkhuni ordination; the nuns there are progressing very well. Venerable Master Wu Yin is noted for the high level of secular and religious education of her nuns. Bhikkhuni Cheng Yen received the Magsaysay Award for starting a hospital for poor people and a medical school. Her charitable organization is so popular in Taiwan that one has to be on a list to do volunteer work there! Another nun, Venerable Hiu Wan literally bought a mountain and built a college for engineering. Slowly she is introducing Buddhist studies in that college. During my visits to Taiwan, I have been very impressed with the nuns, and think that countries that are currently without the bhikkhuni lineage could bring it from Taiwan.

However, due to some problems in the past, a few bhikkhunis in Korea and Taiwan are not very willing to train foreigners as nuns. They say that the Western nuns were too individualistic, making training difficult. It is hard for Chinese and Korean nuns to understand the Western mentality, so steps need to be taken to bridge the gap.

THE BHIKKHUNI ORDINATION

After the Buddha's passing, several Vinaya schools arose. Considering that the *Patimokkha Sutta* in each school was passed down orally for many centuries and that the schools developed in very disparate geographic areas, they are remarkably similar. Naturally, minor differences occur in the number of precepts and in their interpretation. The Chinese follow Dharmagupta Vinaya, which is a sub-branch of Theravada, the tradition followed in Thailand, Sri Lanka, and other Southeast Asian countries. The Tibetans follow Mulasarvastivada.

I am not sure which of these Vinaya lineages the Sri Lankan bhikkhunis brought to China. More research needs to be done to establish this important point. Nowadays there is much discussion about women from countries such as Thailand, Sri Lanka, and Tibet receiving the bhikkhuni ordination from the Chinese community and bringing it back to their own countries, where the lineage of bhikkhuni ordination does not exist at present. However, in general the monks in Sri Lanka and Thailand do not accept the bhikkhuni ordination of the Chinese tradition because it is considered to be from a different Vinaya lineage than theirs. I do not see this as important because all the traditions follow the same general body of Vinaya.

The Buddha said that for Buddhism to flourish in a country, the four groups of Buddhists are needed: bhikkhus, bhikkhunis, laymen, and laywomen. Thus it would be advantageous to bring the bhikkhuni sangha to Buddhist countries where it is not currently present. I think two types of people talk about the possibility of bhikkhuni ordination: the ones who say "no" to it cite a quote from a text and say, "You see, the Buddha never wanted women to join the order." Those who say "yes" to it cite a quote from the same text and say, "You see, it is possible, if you understand the spirit of the precepts." However, indications of change are slowly beginning to appear. For example, in 1998 some prominent Theravada monks participated in a bhikkhuni ordination given by a Chinese master in Bodhgaya, India. Twenty Sri Lankan nuns took the ordination at this time.

Nuns have committed their lives to the Dhamma, and they must not be shy to show others what a positive influence they can have on society. The Buddha's last words were, "Be beneficial to yourself; be beneficial to others." To win the support of society, the bhikkhuni sangha can show that through their Dhamma practice, they benefit themselves by becoming peaceful and happy. They can show that they benefit others by helping them to become peaceful as well. If the nuns come forward and show their capabilities, society will support them. Only then will the conservative monks understand that it is worthwhile for women to join the order. They will see that nuns can help solve many problems and serve others in ways that men cannot do.

APPROACHING THE VINAYA

Initially, only a small number of monks and nuns existed, and since most of them were enlightened, there was no need for a system of precepts. Later, the sangha grew much larger and its members came from more diverse backgrounds. The sangha needed a common set of guidelines for behavior, and thus the Vinaya came into existence. Theravada texts mention ten reasons why the sangha should follow the Vinaya. I have grouped these ten into three major purposes of the Vinaya:

1. To uplift one's own body, speech, and mind. The Vinaya helps each person who joins the sangha to channel his or her physical, verbal, and mental actions in a virtuous direction.

2. To support harmony in the sangha. The sangha consists of people of different castes, social classes, genders, racial and ethnic backgrounds, habits, and values. Without following the Vinaya, such a diverse group could not be harmonious.

3. To confirm the belief of those people who are already Buddhists and to gladden the hearts of those who have not yet become Buddhist. The way an ordained person walks, eats, and speaks influences how people view the Dhamma and the sangha. It helps the general population when they see kind, polite, non-aggressive people. It enhances the faith of Buddhists and helps those who are not yet on the path to come to the path.

Reflecting on these three purposes, we see that the Vinaya is not meant to benefit solely the individual monastic but also the community. For example, if the bhikkhunis follow the Vinaya properly, it will make waves. It will influence the countries that do not have ordained nuns, and the nuns will in turn be appreciated and respected by the larger population.

The Buddha was not a legalist. Each precept was established in response to a specific event. When monastic made a mistake or acted in a way that the lay people found bothersome, it was brought to the Buddha's attention, and he established a precept to guide future disciples in similar situations. In this way, the list of precepts was developed gradually.

Even the Buddha's action was the cause of at least one rule. When the Buddha ordained his son, Rahula, as a novice, the Buddha's father complained. His father was sad because his only son, the Buddha, had become a monk, and now his only grandson, Rahula, was leaving the family life. His father asked the Buddha in the future to ordain young children only with the consent of their parents or guardians, and the Buddha set up a precept in this regard.

It is helpful to divide the material found in the Buddhist teachings into two parts: the teachings dealing with worldly life and those concerning the development of the mind and mental faculties. The latter teachings pertain to everyone. For example, enlightenment is a quality of the mind. It is not related to one's gender, race, and so forth.

On the other hand, the teachings concerning worldly life deal with society and the world, and therefore sometimes speak of the behavior of men and women differently. These teachings can be subdivided into two categories. One corresponds to what was practiced in Indian society at that time. Certain ancient Indian social values were taken into Buddhism, because the Buddhist community was not separate from the general Indian society at that time. Of course, some of these values concerned the position of women. For example, women were to be submissive to men. Spiritual enlightenment was not spoken of in conjunction with women. In India, the only path through which a woman could achieve salvation was *bhakti* or devotion to her husband.

The second category of teachings concerning worldly life shows gender equality. The Buddha came forward and said that a woman can achieve enlightenment. She can be single and does not have to have children. If we look at the formation of the nuns' order and their precepts in the social context of ancient Indian society, we see that the Buddha was ahead of his time when he validated women's spiritual abilities and uplifted their position. By allowing women to be ordained, the Buddha gave women a vision and an unprecedented opportunity that no other religion at that time could offer.

Thus, two types of material are in the Tripitaka, the Buddhist Canon. One clearly supports women. The other seems discriminatory against women due to the incorporation of Indian social values. When we can distinguish between these two types, we can look at Buddhism in a clearer light.

Before the Buddha passed away, he allowed minor precepts to be lifted. However, the elders at the First Council could not decide which precepts were major and which ones minor. As a result, some of the elders proposed keeping the entire body of precepts without changing any.

The first category of precepts, *parajika,* means defeat. If one transgresses any of them, one is defeated in the sense that one no longer is a monastic. The sangha community does not expel that person. Rather, by one's own action one is defeated. Interestingly, monks have four defeats whereas nuns have eight. At the time nuns joined the order, the four defeats for monks were already in existence. The other four were added due to actions of the nuns.

For example, the fifth defeat for nuns says that if a nun feels sexual pleasure from a man stroking upward, lightly touching, squeezing, or holding her in the area from the collar bone down to the knees, she is defeated and is no longer a nun. At first, I did not understand why these actions were serious enough to be considered a *parajika.* Having thought about it for a long time, I see that if both the man and the bhikkhuni feel sexual pleasure, it is like lighting a match. The fire will burn everywhere. If that kind of touching was allowed and sexual pleasure arose, it would be difficult for the two people to stop. That is why the precept is so serious.

How Nuns Can Help Society

Nuns help society simply by being a good example of people who are unpretentious and live in the spirit of non-harmfulness. Aside from their spiritual studies and practice, nuns can also directly benefit society in other ways, one of which is to become involved in issues concerning women. For example, bhikkhunis can help with problems regarding abortion, prostitution, menopause, and other issues that women prefer to discuss with other women. Nuns can also help unwed mothers, many of whom do not want to have an abortion but do not know how to handle the situation. In Thailand, we have just opened a home for women with unwanted pregnancies, so they can avoid abortion and receive the care they need.

Nuns can also help women who suffer after having an abortion. Although as Buddhists, we discourage abortion, some women undergo them. Afterwards, some of these women have regret and confused emotions about their actions. We need to help them accept that this act was committed, teach them means to purify its karmic imprints, and encourage them to go forward in their lives without the burden of a guilty conscience. Some Buddhist women in the West have begun to create rituals to help these women do this.

The nuns' order has great potential, for whatever nuns do will have a ripple effect for Buddhist women all over the world. My hope is that the nuns will use their collective energy to help each other, to contribute to society, and to preserve and spread the precious teachings of the Buddha.

A PRACTICAL APPROACH TO VINAYA

✤

Bhikshuni Jampa Tsedroen

Peter Köst

*B*orn *in Germany, Bhikshuni Jampa Tsedroen worked as a doctor's office assistant. Since 1980 she has studied Buddhist philosophy at the Tibet Center in Hamburg, Germany, according to the traditional Tibetan system under the guidance of Geshe Thubten Ngawang. She was ordained as a sramanerika in 1981, and in 1985 received the bhikshuni vow in Taiwan. From 1988 to 1994, she was the head administrator of the Tibetan Center, as well as a member of the Management Committee of the international Buddhist women's organization, Sakyadhita. She has done extensive research on the Vinaya and is the author of* A Brief Survey of the Vinaya. *Currently she is a lecturer at Hamburg University where she is also working on her Ph.D. in Tibetology. In addition, she studies, translates, and teaches at Tibet Center.*

WHAT IS A PRACTICAL APPROACH TO VINAYA? MY TEACHER, GESHE THUBTEN NGAWANG EXPLAINS IT INVOLVES A GOOD UNDERSTANDING OF KARMA. Although I cannot profess to having this, I have noticed that the more I contemplate karma and the teachings related to it, the stronger my wish to practice Vinaya grows. This leads me to believe that if one has a good understanding of karma and its effects, Vinaya arises naturally.

Some Westerners see Vinaya as merely a system of rules and regulations that exists outside of us. Perhaps this is because, in our limited understanding, we associate Christian monastic discipline with many restrictions. However, in Buddhism, Vinaya is the basis for developing concentration, bodhicitta, wisdom, and all the other realizations of the path. Why? It counteracts two kinds of faults: naturally negative actions and actions prohibited by the Buddha. All naturally negative actions, such as killing as so forth, are a hindrance to the path to liberation because they result in unfortunate rebirths in future lives. In addition, actions prohibited by the Buddha are a hindrance because they prevent good qualities from developing in our mindstream. Thus, following ethical discipline as taught in the Vinaya eliminates hindrances caused by unwholesome behavior and establishes a firm foundation for gaining the higher realizations of the path.

I must study more to understand the complete meaning of Vinaya. However, in the more than fifteen years that I have been learning Buddhism, I have continuously been getting closer to Vinaya practice. The Vinaya contains the means for the way of life that I seek. If we try to behave in accord with the Dharma and look to the Vinaya for guidance, we will find that many important points are explained there. For example, at the end of the *Pratimoksa Sutra,* we find seven guidelines for ending disputes among members of the monastic community. These help resolve conflicts and show how to respect all sentient beings. Vinaya teaches us how to behave in a humble way and how to be satisfied with few things. Rather than try to procure something that is not available, we need to cultivate patience and be satisfied with the situation as it is. Vinaya also instructs us on how to live together harmoniously. In fact, if we understand Vinaya deeply, we can see the entire path to liberation in it.

If we are not able to practice Vinaya, we will not be able to develop a stable meditation practice. Keeping a certain discipline is the basis from which we begin. If we start with high Tantric practices, but lack stable discipline, we are sure to run into difficulties or to harm others or the Dharma. For a beginner such as me, Vinaya is most beneficial, as I can turn to it for practical daily guidelines.

Learning the various precepts is important. There are different categories of precepts according to their gravity: the defeats (*parajika*), the remainders (*sanghavasesa*), and so on. We are not capable of keeping every precept at the beginning. Therefore, the masters advise us to start with avoiding the most serious faults. A practical approach is to learn the main precepts—the defeats and remainders—as soon as we receive ordination. As beginners, we violate precepts each day; as human beings in the desire realm, we cannot altogether avoid violating them. But at least we can minimize the harm and take care not to transgress any of the major precepts completely, thereby losing our ordination. In this way, we can learn one precept after another, first trying to keep the major precepts strictly, and as time goes by following suit with the minor precepts. This is the way the Tibetan monastics train in their communities.

This approach is a natural one, being neither too strict nor too lax. Avoiding these extremes, each person must find for him- or herself the middle way to practice. It is very difficult to keep all the precepts literally, especially at the beginning, and we should avoid having grandiose expectations of ourselves or others. Speaking personally, I feel that I took ordination too quickly, although I do not regret it now. I had practiced the Dharma as a lay person for only one year when I was ordained, and I had to grow and am still growing into a "coat" that is too big for me. I am very fortunate to still be a nun! But I do not suggest that others quickly take ordination as I did. Similarly, I took the bodhisattva and Tantric precepts too early, and now am slowly making the best of it. However, if we took precepts too quickly, we should not regret it later, but understand that at the time we took the precepts we did so with the best motivation of which we were capable. After having taken them, we need to follow them and use the opportunity to learn.

THE GRADUAL APPROACH

At Tibetisches Zentrum in Hamburg, if people want to take ordination, we do not accept their request immediately. Many Westerners want to be ordained just after encountering the Dharma, but I think many of them confuse their strong interest in the Dharma with the need to become a monastic. Many have a romantic view of the monastic life that does not usually have much to do with the reality of living as a monk or a nun in the West.

When people who attend classes at the center request ordination, we usually suggest that first they move closer to the center, continue to work at their job, and attend the seven-year systematic Buddhist study program that we offer. This program is comprised of five years of philosophy covering the four tenet systems, one year of Lamrim (Gradual Path to Enlightenment), and one year of Vinaya and Tantra. Those who do not instantly relate to the philosophy courses can start with the Lamrim and study the other topics later.

We do not require people studying Buddhist philosophy or attending meditation classes at our center to be Buddhists; they can also be Christians and so forth. Presently some psychologists and some university professors who teach comparative religion attend the program. We provide them with the information they need, and that serves their purpose. However, if people come to classes at our center and feel at home with the Buddhist way of thinking, they may become Buddhists if they wish.

When people strongly feel that they would like to become Buddhists, they take refuge by doing the refuge ceremony that our teacher conducts. If they want to take the five lay precepts, we suggest they study the transcripts of the Vinaya lectures of the seven-year program. In these, Geshe Thubten Ngawang gives a general introduction to Vinaya and explains the five lay precepts and other essential points about the Vinaya. After people have read this teaching thoroughly, we ask them to examine whether they are able to keep the lay precepts. If they are, they may take them. Some lay people want to go a step further and take the *brahmacarya* precept, which means that they give up not only sexual misconduct, but also sexual intercourse.

Generally, people can request monastic ordination only after they have finished the seven-year program. This was not the case years ago at our center, which is why I ordained so quickly. However, we have seen or heard of many Westerners who have given their vows back. They left school or their jobs when they ordained, and when they later returned to lay life, they had difficulties because they had not completed their education and so forth. They then remained on the periphery of society. This gives people a bad impression of Buddhism in the West. Since Buddhism is new in the West, if the public comes to think that we train people who then become outsiders in society, the Dharma will not spread.

A CENTRAL LAND

Some Western Buddhists feel that monastics are outdated, that reform is needed, and that the monastic life can be abolished. However, a number of us feel that people should have the opportunity to choose the kind of lifestyle suitable for themselves and thus monasticism should be preserved as a viable option. In addition, monastics can contribute to the existence and spread of the Dharma in society. Indeed, the scriptures explain that for a country to be considered a central land where the Dharma flourishes, the four categories of disciples of the Buddha—the laymen *(upasaka)*, laywomen *(upasika)*, bhikshus, and bhikshunis—must exist. Since we appreciate the Dharma and hope it will remain for a long time, it is therefore important to ensure that these four groups continue to exist.

For me, the process of becoming a bhikshuni was difficult. Initially, I did not know of any bhikshunis in the Tibetan tradition. Before I became a nun, my teacher told me that by taking the novice precepts (sramanerika) I would become a sangha member, but one is allowed to do certain things only when one is fully ordained. Then I heard that Venerable Lekshe Tsomo was trying to find out about full ordination for women and that it might be available in some countries. At that time, I did not feel it was appropriate to raise the question with my teacher because I was busy enough learning the thirty-six precepts.

I was the first person to become a monastic in our center. Later some monks were ordained and they gradually went on to take the full ordination. However, there was no way for me to do that, and for many years I suffered because of this. My teacher is very compassionate and each year we asked His Holiness the Dalai Lama about the research the Tibetans were doing on the bhikshuni ordination. But each year he said that if I was in no special hurry, it would be better to wait one more year. Then in 1985, we asked His Holiness again, and he said, "Now I feel it is the right time to go." I was so happy and said to my teacher, "Now I can go!" But he responded, "Yes, His Holiness said you could, but I do not feel it is good for you to go now." You cannot imagine how much I cried! He said that he felt I did not have the proper motivation. "The correct motivation for going for full ordination," he said, "is renunciation of cyclic existence. You should not seek full ordination because you want to have equal rights with the monks." He knew what he was saying, and because it was true, it was so painful for me to hear. I really suffered. However, gradually I turned my motivation around, and at the end my teacher offered me the air ticket to go to Taiwan to receive the ordination. Subsequently he has helped me so much to learn the Vinaya.

I feel that bhikshuni ordination should be more widely available to those women who sincerely want to take it. Introducing it into the Tibetan tradition would be an enrichment. I no longer see any hindrances to this happening. It is only a question of time, but it will happen. For the Tibetan nuns, it still depends on whether or not they feel they need this ordination. But for Western nuns, I have no doubt. As I mentioned above, the Buddha said that for a country to be a central land where the Dharma flourishes, the four kinds of disciples must be present. If bhikshunis are missing, a place cannot be considered a central land. If they are present in a country as one of the four groups of disciples, then the Dharma can last there for a very long time.

However, we need to take care who enters the monastic community and how its members behave. Monks and nuns need to be well mannered when they interact with society, keeping their precepts and wearing their robes properly. We have seen some Westerners who wear the signs of an ordained person although they have only the five lay precepts. People see them living together with a boyfriend or girlfriend and become confused. If discipline is lax and mixed up like this, the public will no longer know the meaning of being a monastic. For this reason, if someone wants to enter monastic life (Tibetan: *rab 'byung*), we ask them to do it together with the sramanera (male novice) or sramanerika (female novice) vow taken on the same day. In Tibetan society, it is very clear that people who become monastics will leave the household life and their family and enter a monastery. Although they may have to wait for some time to take the novice vow, they enter the monastic life, live in a monastery, and follow the monastic discipline, including abstaining from sexual contact.

If we do not take responsibility for how the monastics behave, the Dharma will be spoiled. Moreover, since many of us Western monastics are pioneers in the place we live, we must be aware that we represent not only the Dharma, but also the Sangha. This is a big responsibility, and His Holiness the Dalai Lama has said that equal rights in the Buddhist community means equal responsibility to study, practice, and preserve the Dharma. This is not always easy, but especially we older monks and nuns need to be clear since we set the standards for everyone else. At the beginning, if the standards are too low, those who come later will be even more lax and the monastic life style will not last very long.

STUDY AND PRACTICE

People often wonder if we can become enlightened without study. We can, but only if we have very strong imprints from our previous lives. Otherwise, it is impossible. People who are able to become enlightened in this very life without having studied the Dharma during this lifetime are very rare, although there are examples of such people historically. Remarkable and auspicious signs generally appeared when they were born, and they usually were noted for being exceptional even as a child. But for the rest of us, who form the vast majority of practitioners, we need to exert effort to learn the Buddha's teachings.

Some people see study and practice as different activities. However, for me they are inseparable. When I study a Dharma text, I feel that I am doing something wholesome. My mind is absorbed in Dharma topics. As I try to understand and contemplate what I am studying, I also relate it to my daily life. For me this is practice, and I cannot imagine spending my time in a better way. In my experience, study supports meditation and meditation solves questions. But meditation also brings up new questions and therefore supports study. So study and meditation go hand in hand.

In debate, we often look at the four possibilities that exist between two things. Let's do this with a Dharma practitioner and a scholar. First, someone could be both. Second, one could be neither. Third, a person could be a scholar but not a practitioner. Such a person would deal with the Dharma only in an intellectual way. Fourth, one could be a realized practitioner but not a scholar, and there are examples of this. In general, I think a good understanding of the Dharma is an enormous aid in practice. For this reason, all the Tibetan traditions have established schools and institutes where the Dharma is learned and taught. Of course, practice is most important. If we study but do not put the Dharma into our hearts, our endeavors are useless.

In our center, the monks and nuns must learn the Tibetan language in the same way that someone who studies theology at the university must learn Latin. However, lay people may do all their studies in German if they wish. Of course, if the monastics try but cannot learn Tibetan properly, we accept that. However, they should try, and since most of them have had a good education and are used to learning languages, they can usually learn Tibetan easily when they attend classes. One nun who has been ordained only one year and a half can already debate in Tibetan. I feel it is important to learn Tibetan since this makes our studies easier and enables us to speak to our teachers directly. By learning Tibetan language, we also learn about the Tibetan culture and way of thinking, which helps us to understand the Dharma better.

The Vinaya instructs that we should not live by ourselves after taking ordination. After taking either the novice vow or the full vow (bhikshu or bhikshuni), we should stay for at least ten years with a teacher who is fully qualified as described in the Vinaya. In brief, the teacher should be venerable, meaning that he or she has been ordained for at least ten years. Second, the teacher should be stable, meaning that he or she has not committed a defeat, or according to some commentaries, has not committed a defeat or a remainder. If someone has, he or she is not considered a pure monk or nun. Third, the teacher should be learned, which is explained in terms of five of twenty-one qualities. In short, the teacher should know the entire Three Baskets: Vinaya, Sutra, and Abhidharma. Fourth, the teacher should be compassionate and genuinely care for his or her disciples.

Once we know the qualities of an excellent teacher, we should look for someone who has them. It is not easy to find such a teacher in these degenerate times. If we cannot find a teacher with all the good qualities, we should find one with at least some of them. According to Vinaya, nuns should be trained by bhikshunis and the monks should be trained by bhikshus. Although this is not always possible now, we should work toward this. For this reason, our center supports the Tibetan nuns doing their *geshe* studies so that we will have female *geshes* and *khenmos* (abbesses) to train other nuns. Each person must decide who her teacher will be; for me a teacher's having the necessary good qualities is more important than their gender.

In our center, after people are ordained, they are asked to take on certain responsibilities. For example, they give talks to the school children when their classes visit the center. They also lead meditation, guide discussion groups, give introductory talks about Buddhism, and so forth. In practice, when asking people to help in various ways we take into account their ability, not only whether they are a monastic. I feel that it is important that not only nuns but also lay people have equal rights and responsibilities. Lay practitioners in the West are different from those in Asia. They are not content with showing devotion to the Buddha shrine and to the Sangha. They want to gain a thorough knowledge of the Dharma. Although only the monastics should perform certain rites, it is fine if qualified lay people give teachings on Buddhism.

The scriptures explain that we have pure Vinaya discipline only if we behave in proper ways with our body and speech, and if we have a good motivation free from defiled attitudes. This points out that we need to abandon the negative emotions. Then, our physical and verbal behavior will naturally become wholesome. If someone were practicing Vinaya perfectly, he or she would be a Buddha, because if one's discipline is perfect, then everything else must be perfect as well.

Every two weeks we do *posadha*, the ceremony to purify and restore our precepts. The Buddha taught this because he knew we are not yet Buddhas and therefore need to purify and restore our precepts. We do not take ordination because we are already highly realized or nearly enlightened, but because we want to learn and practice the Dharma so that we can develop spiritually. In this way, we will become happier and will be able to contribute to the welfare of the greater society by not harming others and by helping them as much as possible.

LIVING AS A BUDDHIST NUN

LIFE IN GAMPO ABBEY—WESTERN STYLE

Bhikshuni Tsultrim Palmo

Bhikshuni Tsultrim Palmo was born in Poland and received a degree in psychology before doing further study in Gestalt Therapy. She raised two children, who are now grown, before she received the sramanerika vows in 1982 and the bhikshuni vows in 1984 in Hong Kong. Beginning in 1986, she did the traditional three-year, three-month retreat at Kalu Rinpoche's center on Saltspring Island, Canada. She served as director of Gampo Abbey in Canada for some years and is now retreat master for the present three-year retreat there.

ESTABLISHING A LIVING PLACE FOR MONASTICS IN THE WEST IS CHALLENGING AND REWARDING. Our community, Gampo Abbey in Nova Scotia, Canada, has gone through many changes over the years. It was founded by Chogyam Trungpa Rinpoche, who escaped to India after the abortive Tibetan uprising against the Chinese communists in 1959. By appointment of His Holiness the Dalai Lama, he became spiritual advisor to the young lama's school which trained the young reincarnate lamas in

India. Rinpoche received a *khenpo* degree, the highest scholarly degree. He then received a Spaulding scholarship and attended Oxford University, where he studied comparative religion, philosophy, and fine arts. He also studied flower arranging and received a degree in it from Sogetsu School. In England, Trungpa Rinpoche started to teach Dharma to Westerners, co-founded the Samye Ling Meditation Center, and learned to speak English fluently. After a car accident, he gave up his monastic robes to avoid Tibetan cultural trappings and the religious fascination of Westerners. He married an English woman and, at the invitation of his Western students, moved to the United States, where he taught at the University of Colorado and developed a friendship with the well-known Zen master Suzuki Roshi. He began to teach widely, establishing the Vajradhatu, Shambhala, and Nalanda organizations, which will be explained later.

In 1983, Trungpa Rinpoche decided to establish a monastic setting for his students and asked people to move to Nova Scotia from Boulder, Colorado. We found a farmhouse and barn on 220 acres on Cape Breton Island, a remote and quiet place. The closest village was a one-hour drive over a mountain. Ane Pema Chodron was asked to lead the abbey, and in 1984, a small group of us, ordained and lay, went to live there. By 1985, the property was paid for in full, freeing us from the burden of a mortgage. Also in 1985, Ven. Thrangu Rinpoche agreed to be our abbot, a position that Trungpa Rinpoche could not take because he was not a monastic. In our name, "Gampo" stands for Gampopa, the student of Milarepa who established monasticism in the Karma Kagyu lineage in the eleventh century and combined the yogic and monastic paths. "Abbey" indicates that it is not a monastery or a nunnery, for monks, nuns, and lay people live there. The nuns and monks practice, study, work, and eat together, although we live in two separate buildings.

Our first monastic program was led by a Chinese bhikshuni, Venerable Yuen Yi, who trained us strictly, but with humor. In subsequent years we were taught by a Western bhikshu, Lama Droupgyu; our abbot, Trangu Rinpoche; the German Theravada nun, Ayya Khema; the scholar, Dr. Herbert Guenther; Jamgon Kongrul Rinpoche; and Ponlop Rinpoche. In 1986, we had our first *varsa* (Pali: *vassa*, Tibetan: *yarney*), the rainy season retreat, and in 1987 we had training in playing Tibetan musical instruments, making *tormas* (ritual cakes), and creating sand mandalas. Since we learned these skills early on and we teach them, we no longer depend on Tibetan lamas to do this. In 1990, the first English language three-year retreat at our retreat center, Sopa Choling, began.

Since 1989, twice a year we have published *The Profound Path of Peace (PPP),* the journal of the International Kagyu Sangha Association of Buddhist monks and nuns. Copies are sent to Kagyu centers worldwide and are positively received.

THE PROGRAM

Our monastic community has grown slowly but steadily over the years. By 1996, we had five bhikshus and four bhikshunis, plus others with lower ordinations. Every year some people take either permanent or temporary ordination. Twenty-four people finished the first three-year retreat (which actually lasted six years because people alternated six-month periods of being in and out of retreat!) in 1996, and the second three-year retreat at Sopa Choling began in 1997. All the Sopa Choling retreatants are ordained for the duration of their retreat. They are in strict retreat and literally separated from the world, including Gampo Abbey, by a fence. The only people authorized to enter the retreat area are the cooks, *druppon* or one who guides the retreat, and maintenance workers.

Bhikshus and bhikshunis, novices, people who are *parmarabjungs* (pre-novices with life-long ordination), and those with temporary ordination all live at Gampo Abbey. Some staff members come for six months or one year to work, practice, and study. In addition, there are program participants and visitors who stay for brief periods of time. Every lay person who comes to Gampo Abbey must take the five precepts, adhere to Gampo Abbey rules, and follow our daily schedule, which includes meditation. Everyone meets regularly with a meditation instructor.

We usually conduct four programs yearly for the general public—three for beginners and one for advanced students. In addition to teachings by Ane Pema Chodron and senior monastics, we invite visiting lamas and other teachers. We do *varsa,* the rainy season retreat, and two one-month *dathuns* each year. During these we meditate for nine or ten hours a day. In 1997, we began a one-month temporary monastic training for young adults ages seventeen to twenty-five. This gives them an alternative to music and drugs by providing intensive training in the Dharma in a monastic setting before they go to college or have a family. We adopted the idea of temporary ordination from the Theravada tradition, and Thrangu Rinpoche gave his consent and began to give temporary vows. Although temporary ordination is common in Theravada countries, it has not been given in the Tibetan tradition before. But we have found that it has a beneficial effect on those who take it, especially the young adults.

Our daily schedule begins with an hour of morning chanting—which includes the *Four Dharmas of Gampopa,* requests to the lineage, and the *Heart Sutra*—and silent meditation at 6:30 A.M. Except for chanting the five precepts in Sanskrit, all other chants and practices are done in English. After breakfast we meditate, either as a group in the shrine room or individually in our room. At 11:00 A.M. there is an optional study period. Everyone keeps silence until noon, when we have lunch. After lunch we work for four hours, and then gather for an hour of meditation and evening chanting. After supper there is a class or silent meditation. Lights go out at 10:00 P.M. Saturday is an unscheduled day, so we can sleep in and do whatever we want. Everyone, including the cook, has the day off. Sunday is all-day practice, and many people meet with their meditation instructor then. We keep silence all day and practice together in the shrine room. Often there is a talk in the afternoon.

Three of our monks are passionate about Dharma study, so our study department is strong and vital. We offer ongoing courses for *shamatha* (the practice to develop concentration) and *ngondro* (preliminary practices), often taught by Pema Chodron. Thrangu Rinpoche visits and teaches at Gampo Abbey about twice a year, and Ponlop Rinpoche and other teachers also instruct us. In 1996, Nythartha Institute, inspired by the monastic colleges, or *shedra*, in Tibetan monasteries, began. Its goal is to transmit the teachings of the Kagyu and Nyingma lineages to advanced Western students.

Gampo Abbey provides an environment and training for people who wish to explore the monastic path. The training has four stages. First one is a candidate. Men or women who are interested in becoming monks or nuns are asked to live in Gampo Abbey for a trial period of at least six months as staff members or as paying guests. Second is pre-novice—*parmarabjung* in Tibetan—a lifetime commitment in which one takes the five precepts: to avoid killing, stealing, unwise sexual behavior, lying, and intoxicants. The *parmarabjung* precept to avoid unwise sexual behavior includes being celibate. Instead of becoming a pre-novice, many people instead take temporary ordination, given for six months to one year, after which they usually leave the abbey and return to lay life. The third stage is being a novice—a sramanera or sramanerika. This ordination is given after the person has been a pre-novice for a year. Taking the novice vow is a lifetime commitment to monastic life. It is held at least three years before progressing to the fourth step, the full ordination as a bhikshu or bhikshuni. When Thrangu Rinpoche gives monastic ordination, the bhikshunis, along with the bhikshus, act as witnesses, a practice not found in the Tibetan community.

MONASTIC RITUALS

As we learn in the Vinaya, there are three important monastic rituals: *posadha, varsa,* and *pravarana.* Since 1984, we have done all of these at Gampo Abbey, and now we use the English translations of these rituals. *Posadha* is done bimonthly, on the new and full moon, and its purpose is to revive virtue and purify whatever non-virtue has been created in connection with our precepts. Because it is a purification rite, *posadha* is done in the morning before eating. It proceeds as follows: the *ghandi,* a wooden instrument used since ancient times to call the sangha for *posadha,* is sounded. We take purification water before entering the shrine room, and then prostrate, recite sutras, and offer *tormas.* The lay people leave the room and contemplate their five precepts in another room. In the shrine room, the monastic leader reads the sutra of discipline, and the *parmarabjungs* and temporary ordained lay people do their confession. They then leave the shrine room and join the lay people. Next, the novices do their confession together and leave. Finally, the bhikshus and bhikshunis perform their confession, after which the *Pratimoksa Sutra* is read. At this point, everybody returns to the shrine room, and we recite the refuge and bodhisattva vows together and take the eight precepts for the day. Next we circumambulate the building—outside or inside depending on the weather—while playing musical instruments, and then return to the shrine room to dedicate the merit.

Varsa is the rains retreat instituted by Buddha Shakyamuni. During monsoon season, to avoid harming the crops and the many insects that grow at that time, monastics did not walk to the villages to collect alms or to teach. Instead, they studied and meditated in one place, usually a garden donated by one of the Buddha's wealthy lay disciples. In this way monasteries or *viharas* slowly evolved. After the rains retreat, some monks stayed in the dwellings to maintain them until the next monsoon, and with time these gatherings grew into communities. In India, the rains retreat lasts three months and is held during monsoon time, in the summer months. In the Karma Kagyu tradition in Tibet, it lasts seven weeks, so at Gampo Abbey we also do it for seven weeks. Initially, our rains retreat was in the summer. However since 1997, it has been in the winter, which is the natural season for retreat in Canada. This is a strict retreat so boundaries are established, and except for people who shop for us, there is no coming and going. There are no telephone calls, no projects, and no work, except for maintaining the abbey. We keep silence and focus on our meditation practice and the study of Vinaya.

The third ritual, *pravarana* is held the last day of the rains retreat. It involves lifting this retreat's special restrictions. Traditionally in Tibet, the nearby villagers came to the monastery the evening before *pravarana*, and the senior monastics gave Dharma talks throughout the night. In the abbey, all the ordained people give talks on the eve of *pravarana*. This is a wonderful opportunity for all monastics to give what is often their first Dharma talk in a friendly, non-critical atmosphere. We are very happy to keep the three essential monastic rituals at our abbey in the West.

PRACTICING THE DHARMA

Our training is both in the Karma Kagyu and Nyingma lineages, and our main meditation practices are *shamatha* and *vipashyana*, or calm abiding and special insight. At Gampo Abbey and Sopa Choling we follow Trungpa Rinpoche's guidelines, designed for Western students. He observed that

Westerners need a solid base of *shamatha*, the calm abiding or tranquillity sitting practice, before starting other meditations. This practice is somewhere between the Theravada-style *vipassana* and sitting *zazen,* and we do it with eyes open. As our main practice, we do it for a minimum of four hours a day.

At Gampo Abbey, as at other Shambhala centers, people do this sitting practice for two or three years. After that, on the recommendation of their meditation instructor, every student attends a three-month course called Vajradhatu seminary. During this course, we study the three vehicles—the Theravada, Mahayana, and Vajrayana—and do *shamatha* practice. At the end, we are given permission to start the first of the Karma Kagyu preliminary practices, prostrations. Each of the *ngondro*, or preliminary practices, is done after finishing the previous one and each practice requires an oral transmission. Three people in our sangha are authorized to give such permission. After finishing the preliminary practices, a person can receive the Annutara Yoga Tantra transmission of Vajrayogini, which was initially given by Trungpa Rinpoche and is now given by his son, Mipham Rinpoche. After finishing the mantras for Vajra Yogini, we can receive Chakrasamvhara empowerment. At this point, we have been practicing meditation for a minimum of six years and are qualified to participate in the three-year retreat at Sopa Choling.

The most wonderful, and most difficult practice, is living in a monastery. For ordained people and those interested in a monastic life, the practice of living a communal life is very powerful. By taking vows we simplify our lives, and this allows us to direct all our energy to the practice of waking up from the sleep of ignorance. The environment and the strict schedule support this, and in that sense, it is easy to live in the abbey. On the other hand, it is very difficult, because we receive instant feedback and see our habitual patterns so clearly. In a monastery there is nowhere to run away, so we must work with our own minds. Our usual habit of blaming others for our pain does not work for long here, because this place is for meditation practice and Dharma study. We are constantly brought back to examine ourselves. When people hear the words "monastery," "abbey," or "nunnery," they often have either a romantic image of a perfect, harmonious, saintly place, or a horrible image of an austere, joyless prison. Gampo Abbey, in reality, is neither. The physical environment is very beautiful, and the people come from different backgrounds and have different personalities. However, they share a common commitment and willingness to work on themselves in order to wake up.

For a while, I was the director of the community. This is also a great practice of serving others and of taking criticism gracefully and responding to it with wisdom. As in all Dharma centers, finding skillful means to communicate is a challenge, as is finding a balance between being too lenient and too strict, between letting people do what they are passionate about and having a real community. Giving commands with "shoulds" and "should nots" does not work with Westerners. They become unhappy and depressed. A leader is challenged to become skillful with people and to help them grow and become softer and less self-centered. There is no general prescription for this; each person has to be dealt with in a different way.

ORGANIZATION

Shambhala is the umbrella organization founded by Trungpa Rinpoche and now led by his son Mipham Rinpoche. It contains three branches: Shambhala training teaches a secular path of spiritual training; Vajradhatu is the Buddhist branch of the organization, in which Gampo Abbey is included; and Nalanda is the branch that brings a contemplative perspective to the arts, health, education, and business. This includes Naropa Institute and the Nalanda Translation Committee.

Venerable Thrangu Rinpoche is the abbot of Gampo Abbey, and we receive instructions, ordinations, and empowerments from him. Similarly, the residents of Sopa Choling receive empowerments for the three-year's retreat from him. Senior bhikshunis and bhikshus are authorized to give temporary ordination. Bhikshuni Pema Chodron is our spiritual director and main resident teacher. Beginning in 1997, we hired a Sopa Choling graduate to be the administrator.

The monastic council and the department heads aid in the administration of the abbey. The monastic council consists of all nuns and monks living at the abbey, including those temporarily ordained. It meets on *posadha* days and makes general decisions about policy and view. Twice a month the department heads gather to discuss finance and construction and to make day-to-day decisions to assure the smooth running of the abbey. Every Monday in a house meeting of all residents, everyone is informed about short- and long-term plans. We exchange opinions and information, introduce new residents, and say good-bye to old residents.

Gampo Abbey is a non-profit organization in Canada and the United States. Our income comes from three sources: 1) donations; 2) programs, visitor fees, and residents' contributions; and 3) royalties from Ane Pema Chodron's books and recordings, fundraising done by monastics, and offerings received from teaching. All monastics live free at the abbey. It is their home and they govern it. Monks and nuns who do not have any income receive a $35 monthly stipend for personal needs. All non-monastic staff are asked to contribute at least $5 daily, if they are able, to help with the food bill.

Our main expenses are food, maintenance, and construction. We have a large garden that supplements our food during the summer. We are vegetarian, but occasionally eat fish. We use wood for heating, and in the near future we will generate our own electricity from a stream on our property.

We plan for monks and nuns to stay, practice, study, and work at Gampo Abbey for hundreds of years. Meanwhile, in the immediate future we will stop the physical expansion and modernization of Gampo Abbey for a few years and concentrate on monastic activities and programs. We will also organize a yearly program for temporary monastics and will continue to study the Vinaya. The three-year retreats at Sopa Choling will continue, as will the Nythartha Institute. We would like to make Ane Pema Chodron's teaching more accessible to the general public by hosting more programs each year, and to propagate the Dharma outside of the Abbey by making ourselves more available for teachings. There is interest in teaching meditation in prisons and working with the dying, as well as in inter-religious dialogue.

Gampo Abbey has a slogan: "Projects are not important—people are." This reminds us that we are here to serve and to practice waking up, not to make an ideal abbey. Living at the abbey brings us down to earth and blows away any sand castles we may have in our minds. Gampo Abbey is a friendly place that has helped many people. We take pride in what has occurred thus far and are extremely grateful for all the wise teachers who have helped us to evolve. Now we look forward with confidence, but also with the knowledge that we have just begun and have a long way to go.

THE THERAVADA SANGHA GOES WEST:
THE STORY OF AMARAVATI

Ajahn Sundara

Born in France, Ajahn Sundara ordained in the Theravada tradition as an eight-precept nun at Chithurst Monastery in England in 1979. In 1983 she received the ten-precept ordination and went to live at Amaravati Buddhist Monastery in England. Subsequently, she resided at Wat Marp Jun in Thailand and recently returned to England to become the abbess of a new nunnery in Devon.

FOR MANY YEARS I HAVE BEEN A MEMBER OF AMARAVATI, A THERAVADA BUDDHIST MONASTERY IN ENGLAND. The story of how our monastic community came into existence is an interesting one. My teacher, Ajahn Sumedho, is an American monk who is the most senior Western disciple of Ajahn Chah, the well-known Thai meditation master from the Thai Forest Tradition who passed away a few years ago. In 1975, Ajahn Sumedho visited London as the guest of the English Sangha Trust, a body founded to establish a Theravada monastic order in England. Inspired by Ajahn Sumedho, the trust members asked their chairman to accompany him back to Thailand and request Ajahn Chah to send some of his Western disciples to reside in England.

Ajahn Chah visited England to access the suitability of the request. In 1977, with his blessings, Ajahn Sumedho and three Western monks fresh from the jungle of northeast Thailand found themselves in a *vihara*, in an urban setting, occupying a town house on a busy street in central London. They started teaching meditation to a few people, and soon more people came to practice with them and to participate in their daily life. Eventually the place became too small, and the English Sangha Trust decided to look for a property outside London.

Meanwhile the monks continued the tradition of going on almsround and used to walk through a beautiful park close to where they lived. One day a jogger who often crossed their path engaged them in conversation. He returned with them to the *vihara*, and after getting to know the monks made them an offer. He had bought a forest in the south of England with the wish to develop and preserve it through modern conservation principles. However, such conservation was beyond his means, and he felt that Buddhist monks, whose philosophy advocated a deep respect for all living things, were the ideal people to take care of it. Thus he offered them the use of that forest. It was an unbelievable gift: a beautiful forest of old English oaks and beeches on about 140 acres of land in one of the most attractive parts of the country.

By a fortunate coincidence, Chithurst House, a large Victorian house nearby, had just been put on the market by the rather eccentric old couple who owned it. The chairman of the Trust made a bid which the couple accepted, and later that year the sangha moved into what would become their forest monastery. They spent most of that first summer, with the small lay community who had joined them, clearing the place of forty years of stuff accumulated by its previous owners.

Most of the monks who originally came to Chithurst had trained in Thailand with Ajahn Chah. At the beginning of this century, Buddhism in

Thailand had turned more into a social institution and lost touch with its roots. It had become the domain of priests and scholars. In reaction to this, some monks chose to return to a way of life close to the one led and advocated by the Buddha. This revival movement, known as the Forest Tradition, brought new breath into Buddhist monasticism in Thailand. The forest monks lived a simple and austere life according to the Vinaya in solitude in the forest and devoted themselves to the practice of meditation and the realization of the Buddha's teaching. It is remarkable that a tradition so remote from our materialistic Western culture has been transplanted to the West, and within a relatively short time, has integrated itself into society. In the towns near our monasteries, the sight of monks or nuns on almsround is now familiar.

I arrived at Chithurst in September of that first year. I had just returned from abroad when a friend told me that the monks had moved out of London. I was very busy, but three days later I traveled to Chithurst, curious to find out what was happening at the monastery. I was then a lay person more interested in meditation than in Buddhism itself. Earlier that year I had done a retreat with Ajahn Sumedho, and at the end, when someone had asked me if I wanted to be a nun, I had replied that maybe, when I was seventy and there was nothing left to do. With that frame of mind, I arrived at Chithurst, talked with Ajahn Sumedho, and told him that life and the world were great. Sure the world was full of problems, but it was challenging and that's what I loved about it. He just said, "Yes, but it depends where the world is." Something in me stopped. I had read numerous times and been told that the world originated from the mind, but I was living my life as if the world were "outside." At that moment the understanding lasted just a millisecond. I did not become conscious of the profound effect his insight had on me until three weeks later I realized that I was still at Chithurst! Many doubts had fallen away, and I felt an incredible confidence and inner freedom. I was aware that I had choice: the world was not "out there," so it was up to me to live my life the way I wanted.

I loved the lifestyle of the retreat I had attended previously: eating one meal a day, getting up early in the morning, and meditating throughout the day. I also valued the silence, the reflections on Dhamma, and having time to think for myself rather than to read books or listen to others' ideas. So I thought, "Why not carry on in a similar environment for a while?" I still did not think of becoming a nun, but I was confident that spending a few months in a monastic environment and keeping the eight precepts could only be beneficial. I wanted to understand my mind and how it was possible to make peace with it. I had a taste of this during a previous retreat and realized that even for a short time, not contending with myself or the world around me had wonderful effects on my life. At thirty-two, I felt that it was time to find out how I wanted to spend the next fifty years, for it seemed that life was going very fast and there was a real sense of urgency.

Thus I decided to stay at Chithurst. However, this new situation was quite a challenge. Three other women had come to live there also. We did not know each other and came from different backgrounds and different countries. I must confess that even though I had good women friends, I did not like women very much and in general got along much better with men. Also, living within the restraint of the eight precepts, I could not eat after noon or sleep as long as I liked. A great part of the day was spent in Chithurst House which was then a busy work site—cold, dark, and dusty. My temperament was to love beauty, comfort, and clean places! Cooking had never been my favorite pastime, yet I found myself cooking for twenty-five people almost every day in a marquee—a large tent that had been turned into a kitchen. It was full of wasps, and normally it took only one to get me really agitated. But somehow they did not bother me, and I was very happy in spite of all the new challenges, or more likely, because of them.

Shortly after arriving, we became *anagarika*, or eight-precept nuns. A special ceremony marked our "official" entry into the community. Wearing the traditional white robes of Thai *maechees* (nuns), and with our hair cropped—we started shaving our head a year later—we formally took the eight precepts in the presence of the monastic community and some friends and were given a new name in Pali. The community consisted then of six monks, four nuns, and a few laymen.

The forest at Chithurst was extremely beautiful and quiet. In the early years, even though we had periods of silent formal practice, most of our energy was spent working on the house that had to be rebuilt inside almost from scratch. In those days a pioneering energy gave the community great impetus and strength to go through difficulties and obstacles with faith. Our daily schedule was in many ways similar to that of Thai forest monasteries. We got up at 4:00 A.M. and walked in the dark from our cottage to the main house to attend morning puja. During the morning we worked in the kitchen, the garden, or the office. The monks continued the tradition of going on almsround while the rest of the community was busy building or working in the forest. Our main meal was at 10:30 A.M. Afterwards we had a rest period and worked all afternoon. After a hot drink and a short break, we gathered for evening puja. Once a week we had a quiet day, a kind of Buddhist Sabbath, which was followed by an all night meditation practice. This schedule has remained more or less the same up to the present, although now there is less physical work, and lay people help us to run the monastery so that we have more time to focus on "inner work." Initially, just keeping pace with the schedule was a difficult discipline. Having been a dancer, however, I was used to strong physical training. Interestingly, I felt more energetic than before because my energy was not wasted in endless distractions. Ajahn Chah would tell people who were lethargic in meditation, "Sleep little, eat little, and talk little." How true this is!

Entering into Practice

When I came to the community, I did not know the Buddhist scriptures. I was mainly interested in living my life with integrity so that when it ended I would have no regrets. This motivation has given me great incentive throughout my monastic life. Before long I saw, even at a modest level, that it was possible for the mind to abandon negative habits, be truly peaceful, and respond to life from a place of freedom and compassion. This encouraged me to investigate and understand the mind at a deeper level. Training of heart, understanding of Dhamma, and working to realize liberation were clearly ongoing processes, a lifetime's work that could not be done in just a few months!

Meditation was and still is the foundation of this life. It gave me the clarity with which to look within and see the mind as a mirror. The practice is focused on the teachings of the Four Noble Truths, which in the Theravada tradition is considered one of the most important teachings for realizing nibbana, the goal of the Buddhist teaching. Through awareness of our suffering and understanding of its cause—the first and second Noble Truths—the Buddha teaches that we can let go of the basic illusion that we are a self, an ego. As we keep watching inwardly—thoughts, feelings, the body and its sensations, perceptions, and mind (the five *khandas*)—we need not be limited or bound by our identification with our body or our mind. By observing again and again how impermanent, painful, and empty of self they are, we can let go of our attachment to and identification with them. Actually, it is more correct to say "there is letting go," because we cannot find anyone that lets go. This letting go experience is called the third Noble Truth and must be realized. The development of the path is the fourth Noble Truth or Noble Eightfold Path. It is a detailed guide to practice, which is quiet inner work, nothing dramatic. Sustaining mindfulness and a clear vision of the experience in the present moment is important, practice focuses on all aspects that generate, strengthen, and sustain mindfulness. This brings about the wisdom that can break through the delusion of the mind. Outwardly, we use the monastic ethical standard to guide our verbal and physical actions. Slowly, we harmonize the energies of our mind and body by not recreating unskillful behaviors, which are the main sources of our inner conflicts. It is not enough to know that the Four Noble Truths exist. For them to become the Truths that the Buddha realized, we have to gain profound insight into the nature and reality of the mind.

I was amazed that in the midst of a real intense and painful situation, my heart could often remain joyful. Meditation taught me that the suffering I experienced was not a trap anymore but a source of learning. I now had the necessary tools to transform this human experience of greed, hatred, delusion, and selfishness. By looking directly into the mind at the nature of that experience—its impermanence, unsatisfactory nature, and selflessness—it was possible to let go of the blind habit that kept grasping it. Why do we hold on to suffering? Because at some level we do not understand what it is and how it affects the heart. If we knew, we would drop it straight away. As I observed again and again how little control the mind has over its suffering, it became obvious that pain is not "mine." What a relief it was to discover that we do have a method to get out of our predicaments!

Prior to joining the community, I avoided the unpleasant sides of life and did not talk about anger, frustration, and selfishness. Harmony, love, philosophy, and art were so much more interesting to me. But, practicing Dhamma, I had to look at the ugly things in myself. People living with me became clear reflections of my mind, and without the social screens we usually put up to alleviate pain, there was no way to hide any more. I kept bumping into this self with its selfishness, anger, pettiness, fear, impatience and so forth. Previously, I thought I was kind, open-minded, and easygoing. But when I looked, I saw how critical and judgmental I was. What a surprise that was!

It was Buddhism's practicality and relevance to everyday life, not its philosophy, that appealed to me. The practice and the material I was working with were tangible, and I was not interested in reading books. Monastic life was so much more alive than anything I had ever encountered. Often, nothing much seemed to be happening externally, but inwardly, I would be going through a powerful cathartic process. Without a deep commitment to the practice and to the Buddha, Dhamma, and Sangha as refuge, it would have been difficult to transverse those times.

The style of training in this tradition is very appealing to me. Initially, we do not need to study a lot. The monastic environment itself demands that we be alert and mindful. We rapidly learn how the law of cause and effect works at a grassroots level. We discover that if we are not careful, we receive the results of our actions immediately. Also, in community, although we no longer have the usual outlets for our creativity, we discover that this creative energy continues in the most mundane situations and activities. When we were novices, for example, cooking became the field of our artistic creations! My imagination would go wild as I prepared an elaborate meal in no time. But this was not the way to peace! When others cooked, I witnessed my critical mind: "These people can't cook! They are hopeless! They can't even cut carrots properly!" In that environment, all my buttons got pushed, and I could be so righteous. I had to train myself to repeat a mantra—"Let go, let go"—all morning while working in the kitchen. I had to concentrate, because in just one moment of heedlessness I would lash out at someone. Sometimes greed would fuel my energy. In that situation the absurd was so obvious that I could clearly see my attachments and how miserable they made me. We need a good sense of humor to recognize and let go of these things.

Every week we practice sitting and walking meditation through the night. Imagine what the mind can conjure up at the prospect of not sleeping all night! It plays every possible trick to justify going to sleep or it creates good, even inspiring reasons to justify the validity of staying up. Sometimes our pride keeps us awake because we have energy to check on others and criticize them, "Look at that one dozing off! How disgusting and shameless!" The judgment lasts until we find ourselves exhausted and join the sloth and torpor lot. Monastic training does not allow us to lie to ourselves for long time because we are in an uncomfortable environment, where people often drive us up the wall and our basic survival mechanisms are challenged. In this setting, the teaching is a constant encouragement to observe our reactions to life with gentleness and love. We discover that just changing our attitude enables us to develop qualities that strengthen and liberate the heart. We tap into an extraordinary reserve of energy when we live this life wholeheartedly. After a while, we experience the mind when it is not preoccupied with itself. It is free, even for a short time, of its inner turmoil; it becomes bright, filled with peace and love.

WOMEN IN THE COMMUNITY

More women joined our little community at Chithurst, and by 1983 we were eight *anagarikas* (practitioners with eight precepts). We came from different European countries but shared a similar strong aspiration to practice the Dhamma within a monastic form. In Thailand, Ajahn Sumedho hardly had any contact with nuns. Having women in Chithurst and teaching them was a new experience for him. I don't think he quite knew what to do with us at first, so we took responsibility for our own training. We were keen on the discipline, which we knew played an important role in transforming the mind. Ajahn Sumedho could see that we were serious about pursuing this way of life and began to consider how women in the West could further their training beyond the traditional form of Thai *maechees*. In Thailand, women who wish to live in a monastery shave their head, take the eight precepts, and support themselves materially. They are in a rather ambiguous situation: although they are nuns, they do not benefit from the advantages and support traditionally given to the ordained sangha. They primarily support the monks' community, especially by cleaning the temple and preparing the monks' daily meal. Currently, however, new models for Thai nuns are emerging that allow them to learn the Dhamma and to train and practice outside the traditional *maechee* role.

Seeing that European women were serious about practice and would benefit from training similar to that of the monks, Ajahn Sumedho asked permission from the Elders in Thailand to initiate the ten-precept ordination for women. He received their blessing to do so, and in 1983 the four of us who had joined the community in 1979 received the ten-precept ordination in the presence of the bhikkhu sangha and hundreds of people who came to witness this auspicious event. We received a set of brown robes—the robe material being offered by Thai lay supporters—and a beautiful ceramic almsbowl. The latter came as a surprise, as we did not know that we would use a proper almsbowl and were delighted at the thought of going on almsround.

The ten-precept ordination was a major step. It opened to women in the Thai Theravada tradition a way of life and a training quite similar to the one followed by the nuns during the Buddha's lifetime. This monastic form, based on the ten precepts, made us totally dependent upon the generosity and kindness of others. Through the years this form has evolved in an organic way. There were no models, no precedent to follow. The bhikkhuni order established by the Buddha had died out in the Theravada tradition some fifteen hundred years ago. Thus no lineage had remained for women who wished to live and train following a way of life based on alms-mendicancy, which in the Forest Tradition implies the relinquishment of money and thus of independence on the physical level. On Ajahn Sumedho's part, it was a true act of faith to establish this training for women as many "reasonable" questions could have prevented it from coming about: Would this traditional form be suitable for Western women? Would it be accepted by the society? Would women monastics in the West be supported as monks have been for the last twenty-five centuries?

For the first year after taking the ten precepts, we followed the traditional Theravada training of a *samanera*. However, unlike the expansive Vinaya for bhikkhunis, the ten precepts did not deal with many areas of our life. We realized that to live together as a group, we needed to have a common understanding of the precepts, the use of requisites, and many other practical aspects of our daily life. Therefore, we gathered materials from various sources with the help and guidance of a senior monk, Ajahn Sucitto. We selected rules most appropriate to our life from the *samanera* training and the bhikkhu and the bhikkhuni Vinayas and rewrote them in modern language. In this way, we prepared a Vinaya book and a recitation of the training rules, which we do fortnightly. We also formulated the procedure for clearing the transgressions of our precepts. In this way, we researched the nuns' monastic life and found that the bhikkhuni Vinaya developed twenty-five centuries ago deals with issues and behavior relevant to our community. Using this discipline to train our body and our speech has proved very effective in helping the mind to relinquish its self-cherishing interests, delusion, greed, hatred, and the idea that we are a permanent self. The discipline also promotes harmony because we follow agreed-upon standards. Instead of spending hours discussing the best way to do this or that, we turn to the Vinaya for advice and benefit from the wealth of experience and wisdom of this discipline.

By 1983, our cottage at Chithurst had reached its full capacity, and several other women were waiting to ordain. Plans were made to find a new place, and a year later Amaravati Monastery was established in Hertforshire,

LIVING AS A BUDDHIST NUN

England. In 1984, the nuns moved to Amaravati. To celebrate this auspicious event we decided to go there on foot, following an ancient practice of Buddhist renunciants called *tudong* in Thailand. This practice is usually undertaken by monks to face new challenges and test themselves after their initial period of training. In England, this has become a regular feature of our life, and every year monks and nuns go on *tudong*. We walk, carrying our bowl and a few belongings, around Britain, Ireland, or other European countries. Sometimes we go in a group of two or three, accompanied by an *anagarika* or a lay friend, and other times we travel on our own without money. We depend on whatever people offer us for our daily meal and material necessities. It is a journey in faith, we never quite know what the next day will bring and are instantly brought into the present moment. Although it may be difficult at times, many of us have found this experience to be rewarding and joyful. In addition, most of the people we meet on the way are friendly and are inspired to see monks and nuns still living on faith.

Our *tudong* to Amaravati took three weeks. Upon our arrival, we were welcomed by the sangha and the lay community who had come to join in this happy occasion. Our new dwelling place was located on top of a hill under a vast open sky. It had originally been a school and was a large complex of wooden buildings. Like Chithurst, it was in a very attractive part of the country. Large enough to accommodate many people, it offered an excellent situation for hearing and practicing the Dhamma and for a wide spectrum of activities. We now have a retreat center, a large library, summer camps for families and children, regular meditation workshops, seminars, and interfaith gatherings.

After receiving guidance and Vinaya training from Ajahn Sucitto for a few years, we nuns became more experienced and confident in using the ten precept form and took responsibility for the running of our own community. This was an important shift, for until then we had been emulating the male community and had adapted a hierarchical model. When we became more autonomous, we learned to work together in tune with the needs of female monastics. We had to assume many responsibilities, a challenging process as none of us had much experience in this way of life. For the last few years, the senior nuns have overseen the training of the junior members and offered them guidance and support in their Dhamma practice. We have also managed the affairs of the community and shared the administrative duties and responsibilities of the monastery. We regularly receive invitations to teach and to lead retreats in England and abroad. By 1986, seventeen nuns and novices lived in the two nunneries of Chithurst and Amaravati. Recently, a third place—the first experiment of a totally autonomous nunnery—has been established in Devon.

It is still too early to anticipate how our community of nuns will evolve in the future. We have learned that this is always wonderfully uncertain. But the seed has been planted and through the deepening of our trust in the Dhamma, it will continue to be nurtured and will bring many fruits for the benefit and happiness of all beings.

BLOSSOMING IN PLUM VILLAGE

Bhikshuni Tenzin Namdrol

Born in Rio de Janeiro in 1934, Bhikshuni Tenzin Namdrol met the Dharma in 1974 after returning with her five sons to Brazil from Mozambique, her adopted country. In 1987 she began to study with Zopa Rinpoche in India and later opened the Dorje Jigje Center for Buddhist Studies in Rio de Janeiro. Ordained as a sramanerika in 1996, she resided at Gampo Abbey before going to Plum Village in 1998 to receive bhikshuni ordination from Thich Nhat Hanh. She plans to return to Plum Village in 2000 to begin a five-year monastic training program.

PLUM VILLAGE CONSISTS OF SEVERAL HAMLETS PERVADED BY THE PRESENCE OF THICH NHAT HANH, OR THAY AS HE IS CALLED BY HIS DISCIPLES. The air in this part of France is crystal clear, and the rolling landscape dotted with old farms delights the eye. In summer Plum Village is filled with visitors, and children enjoy the swings, seesaws, sandbox, and tree houses on the grounds. In winter the premises are quieter, and the monastics do retreat.

Lower Hamlet comprises seven buildings individually housing nuns, single women, couples and children. A small zendo, service areas, library, shed, bookstore, and one large zendo or meditation room also fill the cluster. To hone the notion of community, nuns and single women are assigned three to a room regardless of how many empty rooms exist. No furniture other than beds is in the bedrooms, and all belongings are kept in a large common room. In the common study, we each have our own bookshelves for study materials. The buildings lack sound insulation, and the floors are made of hollow planks, but we hear no feet treading and no chatter except on "lazy days," the one day each week when no tasks except cooking are done.

New Hamlet consists of a manor house shared by Vietnamese and Western nuns, lay women, and the Vietnamese abbess. It has two beautiful, small zendos and a large one in the meadow. Upper Hamlet stands on a flat hill surrounded by grassy fields and woods containing meditation cabins. Here monks and lay men live. Each hamlet has a rectangular zendo where over three hundred people can easily sit.

In the nuns' house at Lower Hamlet live Sister Abbess and eleven Vietnamese nuns: eleven are bhikshunis and one is a novice. The abbess, Sister Jina, a European well versed in both Western and Eastern traditions, is well loved and respected. The sangha lives as one precept body, forming individuals into a true community that makes decisions and shares responsibilities. This close communal living brings much freedom and joy to each member and makes refuge in the sangha a powerful part of our daily lives.

The nuns are the core of the community. Reminded to use skillful means to work out personal differences, they manifest joy and trust in one another, thus setting the tone for the rest of the community. All tasks and chores are rotated and accomplished by groups of five or six practitioners led by a nun. Each group cooks once a week, the only person exempt from this task being the abbess. Hers is the only set position; all others are changed periodically. If a sister is especially gifted in an area she may be assigned to a project in which that skill is needed. However, once the project is completed, she rejoins the pool of sisters and is assigned to another job. Mindfulness practice quickly appeases our speedy habits. Nuns are expected to handle a multitude of tasks demanding training in such varied fields as art, computers, rituals, singing, and public speaking. Nevertheless, no one appears burdened by any task, and no one is irreplaceable. Closed offices where specialists remain on working binges are absent in Plum Village. The nuns are humble, educated, well balanced, and cheerful.

MINDFULNESS IN DAILY LIFE

Our practice centers on continuous mindfulness in which we pay attention and bring joy to each activity. Work is done in silence, and when the mindfulness bell rings, we pause and breathe mindfully three times before returning to whatever we were doing. Walking anywhere—from the table to the sink, to and from our house—is done slowly and mindfully, bringing body and mind in harmony regardless of the chores we are carrying out. When the phone rings, which is constantly during the day and several times during meals, we stop what we are doing, are mindful of our breath, and answer the phone with a smile after the third ring. Every fifteen minutes clocks chime, and again we stop to focus on our breath, resuming whatever we were doing when the chimes stop. When we talk, we don't walk; when we walk, we don't talk. We do one thing at a time, always mindfully. Mindfulness opens our hearts to the here and now; we discover within ourselves infinite gratitude for life, as well as for the soil we tread and the oxygen we breathe. Mindfulness transforms our careless, self-centered ways into gentle, loving ones.

We are trained to be attentive to our interactions with each other. During the fine manners class, inspired by Stepping into Freedom, a book of monastic conduct, we learn to respect others and to actively demonstrate that respect. For example, before and after addressing any monastic, we gasho or bow to the person. We do this as well before sitting down for a meal or meditation. We learn and practice kitchen manners, dining room manners, bathroom manners, and zendo manners, making life pleasant and caring. These rituals lend sacredness to our lives.

Beauty and music are important at Plum Village. Many of Thay's poems have been set to music, and monks and nuns often sing together. The Heart Sutra has been set to a simple melody, and by chanting it every morning, we carry the tune in our hearts throughout the day.

The day begins with a bell at 5:00 AM, and a half-hour later we meet for chanting and walking meditation. At 7:00 AM, we return to our rooms for individual practice until the bell is invited for our simple but scrumptious breakfast, prepared by that day's cooking team. In the evening after the day's cleaning team has finished its work, the bell is invited again for evening meditation and liturgy until almost 10:00 PM. We are never tired, and time flies.

Twice a week Thay gives teachings in one of the hamlets, which hosts the others. A youthful 72, Thay is a simple monk, as His Holiness the Dalai Lama also likes to call himself. Permanently in a deep state of mindfulness, he glides slowly into the zendo, followed by two monks or nuns, who are never the same. He sits on a cushion on a elevated platform before a low lectern when teaching, but he also walks about and writes on a large board, sometimes sitting sideways on the platform. His simplicity, in contrast to the sophisticated PA system, makes Thay appear accessible, although he seldom addresses anyone personally and does not allow time for questions. Every few weeks, however, he announces "Dharma a la carte" in which questions collected from his students form the basis for the day's teachings. When teaching, he speaks first in Vietnamese, with simultaneous translations done by his students into English and French. Then he speaks in either French or English, with simultaneous translations into the other languages. Groups of Germans, Italians, Spaniards, and others improvise their own translations.

After the teachings, we form a circle outside to sing simple Dharma songs, followed by a forty-five minute walking meditation led by Thay. Lunch is formal: we sit according to a strict seating arrangement, eat in silence, and use our begging bowls. Meals can take a long time since we are often interrupted by various bells and rings, each prompting us to pause and breathe mindfully three times. In the afternoon, we meet for either a tea meditation or a Dharma discussion, and in the evening we gather again for meditation and chanting until 10:00 PM.

COMMUNITY

The Plum Village sangha comprises approximately one hundred monks and nuns, with about sixty living in Plum Village and forty in Maple Forest Monastery in Vermont. Before receiving the first vows, candidates live in Plum Village to experience the lifestyle for several months. In this way, they can determine if it is appropriate for them, and the community can also see if a candidate is sufficiently prepared for monastic life. The sense of community is strong, and only ten percent of the monastics have disrobed. Thay attributes this, as well as the spread of his teachings, to the support a harmonious sangha offers each practitioner, and he devotes a great deal of time and talent to cultivate this.

Of course, not everyone is suited for or can adjust to such intense communal life. These people usually discover this and depart within a few days. Those who do not are asked to write a letter of intent, which is periodically reviewed. After some time, it may become evident that a different environment would be more beneficial.

Liturgy is meaningful and carefully prepared. Thay often recommends changes in the liturgy and prepares new rituals for special use. The "beginning anew" ceremony is an example of this. Here, we sit in groups of about ten and share the specific ways in which our fellow practitioners have nurtured us or caused us difficulties. This is a time for deep listening, expressing gratitude, and improving our communication. Our morning liturgy begins with a series of prostrations to the Three Jewels, several bodhisattvas, spiritual lineage, and ancestors and is followed by a formal reading of the five mindful trainings—the five Buddhist precepts updated and reworded by Thay to stimulate our mindful living. On other days, formal ceremonies to purify and renew the novice or the bhikshuni vows are held. We often read sutras or chant while doing walking meditation together. In short, all the occasions we meet together benefit the individual as well as the community.

Thay integrates Buddhism into a universal and personal practice for peace, and thus when we bow to the spiritual lineage we may include Jesus and Mary if we wish. Medals of both Jesus and Avalokiteshvara are placed on the patriarch's table during Christmas, which is elaborately celebrated with an enormous tree, presents for everyone, wreaths, thousands of home-made cookies, and special meals. Thay talks about the common roots of the Christian and Buddhist traditions, a teaching everyone relishes. Hanukah is also celebrated in a moving way, leading one lady from Israel to comment that this was the first time the holiday had deep meaning for her.

Thrift, a significant factor for a people not yet healed from a devastating war followed by poverty and famine, is emphasized in the community. Water is precious and consumed mindfully at all times. Electricity is also used mindfully, and unnecessary lights are turned off. We have washing machines but no dryers. Although the original buildings have been weatherproofed and lovingly preserved, for warmth in the public rooms we rely on layers of clothing, scarves, wool caps, and gloves. But it is with food that we best learn frugality, for not even a grain of rice is ever lost. Pots and serving dishes are scraped, with leftovers kept in a cabinet for use the same day. Food is simple, varied, plentiful, and cooked lovingly.

Although to the common eye monastics at Plum Village may appear disempowered—they have no personal money, relinquish preferences, and must request permission to leave the premises (and if it is granted, they always go out accompanied)—our experience is one of enormous freedom, space, and trust. Of course, there are differences of opinions and feelings are sometimes hurt, but the simply courtesy which is a natural outcome of ongoing mindfulness training enables us to restore balance. Dharma is integrated into every aspect of life in the community, and from this we learn that the Dharma is truly the only medicine which can temporarily and ultimately dispel all suffering.

RESTORING AN ANCIENT TRADITION:
THE LIFE OF NUNS IN MODERN MAINLAND CHINA

Bhikshuni Ngawang Chodron

Born in London, Bhikshuni Ngawang Chodron was a photographer. In 1977, she received sramanerika vows from Trulshik Rinpoche and studied with Dilgo Khyentse Rinpoche. She received bhikshuni ordination in Hong Kong in 1987 and studied under her bhikshuni upadhayayini *in Mainland China. She lives at Shechen Tannyi Dargyeling Monastery in Nepal and is currently involved in establishing a nunnery for Tibetan nuns in Nepal.*

Martine Frank/Magnum Photos

Few people know about the lives of the nuns in Mainland China, and I was fortunate to learn about it from direct experience. As bhikshunis, one of our precepts is to follow our *upadhayayini*—a senior bhikshuni who trains a new bhikshuni and acts as her role model—for two years. In 1987, when I became a bhikshuni, no one in the Tibetan tradition could fulfill that role where I lived. Thus I went to Hong Kong where I met a bhikshuni from China whom I admired. Although I could not speak Chinese and she could not speak English, I asked her through an interpreter if I could be her disciple. She modestly replied that she had learned nothing, but I took this as a sign of her humility and my respect for her grew.

In 1994, I went to her temple in China for the summer retreat. Later I went with her to Jiu Hua Shan, the holy mountain of Kshitigarbha, for a large ordination ceremony where she was the chief instructor for the 783 bhikshunis ordained at this time. When we consider the extensive harm that the communist regime has inflicted on Buddhists and Buddhist institutions in the last four decades, it is remarkable and wonderful that so many women in China now want to be ordained.

The first year I spent in China was difficult because I did not know Chinese. Although I tried hard to do everything with the nuns, I could not keep up. To learn Chinese I would write a Chinese character and ask someone to tell it to me in *pinyin*, the phonetic system for Chinese. In this way, I learned the characters for some key words and was able to follow the text when they chanted. Unfortunately, the weather was so hot that I became ill and could not study Chinese regularly.

In 1995, I spent the summer retreat at my master's nunnery in Guangzhou. Following that, we attended another large ordination at Wu Tai Shan, the holy mountain of Manjushri, where three hundred bhikshunis and three hundred bhikshus joined the order. My stay in China then was easier because I knew some Chinese, and interestingly, I did not feel like a foreigner. I wore Chinese robes and felt very comfortable with the nuns. Sometimes the Chinese nuns wanted to try on my Tibetan robes and asked me to take their pictures when they did!

THE BEAUTY OF MONASTIC DISCIPLINE

Early in their training, the nuns are taught to stand like a candle, walk like the wind, sit like a bell, and sleep like a bow. Chinese people are concerned that things look good, and some of my actions, which seemed fine to me, provoked reprimands. As a foreigner, it was very difficult to know what looked good and what did not, especially when it came to minor actions such as how to wash one's clothes. I had some trouble with these cultural differences, until I learned what we were supposed to do.

Quite a number of women came to my master's nunnery in Guangzhou to ask to become nuns. First they were interviewed by the abbess, and if she thought they had the necessary qualifications, she would take them in. They then spent two years as lay devotees in the nunnery. These women—most of them young—came with long hair, which was cut short, and wore the long black robe during the chanting services. They usually worked in the kitchen or in the garden because the nuns are not allowed to dig the ground or weed as this could harm insects.

One of the first things told to young women entering the nunnery is, "You have to *ting hua*," meaning, "You have to obey." This is very important, and the new nuns diligently follow the instructions of their seniors. After they have been at the nunnery for at least two years, have studied the sramanerika precepts, and are well trained, they are allowed to receive the sramanerika ordination.

Later, when they are ready, they attend a triple ordination platform, at which time they receive the sramanerika, bhikshuni, and bodhisattva vows. This program includes a rigorous three-week training period. The smartest nuns, who know proper behavior, are put in front and lead the other novices. Everybody is taught how to wear their robes, walk, eat, stand in line, bow, use the sitting mat—all that they need to know during the ordination and during their lives as nuns. They also learn how to live the Vinaya in daily life and memorize verses to recite when they awake in the morning, put on their robes, tie their belt, go to the toilet, and so on. In those weeks all kinds of individuals from all parts of China and every walk of life learn the same basic monastic behavior.

My master's nunnery is well known for its study. Everyone attends morning prayers that begin at 3:30 A.M. Afterwards we study until breakfast, which according to Vinaya must be eaten after it is light enough to see the lines on our palm. We wear our full, formal robes in the dining room and eat in silence. After breakfast, we recite a sutra, do necessary work at the nunnery, and attend a class on the precepts. Before lunch we make offerings to the Buddha in the main hall, and then file into the dining room for the main meal of the day. After lunch, everybody rests, this afternoon nap being very sacrosanct! In the afternoon we chant the sutras, make another offering to the Triple Gem, and then attend another precept class and small study groups.

The Chinese nuns have a strong sense of community, fostered by an atmosphere of equality and respect. For example, everybody, including the abbess, receives the same amount of the same food. Everyone also does some sort of work for the communal well being. One group takes care of the grounds and the temple. Another does kitchen duty, which is a lot of work and no fun, but everybody works together. Of course, in any group of people, factions exists, but the nuns are very generous and not possessive of what they have.

In fact, the nuns are extremely disciplined and do not want to have possessions. For example, the abbess said I could have meals in my room, because it was difficult for me to wear the formal robes in the hot, crowded dining hall. One of the most exemplary nuns in the temple brought my food. I wanted to give her a gift to thank her, but there was nothing she wanted even though the nuns have very little in their rooms. Instead, they want to give to other people. For example, when an ordination occurs, they bring their clothes to give to the new nuns. They enjoy doing things for others, thus creating a wonderful sense of community.

When a bhikshuni shaves the head of a nun and takes that novice on as a disciple, she is responsible for that nun. She must ensure that the new nun has food, clothes, housing, and teachings in the future. When my master received special offerings from donors, she gave them to her disciples. When those things were gone and she had little left, she gave them her own clothes. The disciples are also responsible to their master and greatly respect her. They care for her, help her with Dharma projects, and practice as she instructs.

The Chinese nuns who have the opportunity to study in nunneries appreciate this very much. They follow the Dharmagupta Pratimoksa as strictly as possible, so discipline is strong. Although conditions necessitate that they handle money, which is technically prohibited in the nuns' precepts, they recite a verse requesting purification before taking the money. They do not eat after lunch; if they need to take some medicine or liquid later, they recite a verse to another bhikshuni who responds with the verse of approval. They use the discipline in the Vinaya to strengthen their awareness in daily life activities. For example, before eating they remember that as monastics, they should be worthy of the food that the sponsors offer to them. They recall not to eat it with greed, but to regard it as medicine which sustains the body for the purpose of practicing the Dharma.

Further, no nun will go out alone. Once I had to empty the garbage two steps outside the nunnery, and one nun would not let me. Of course, since so few bhikshunis live in the West, going out with another bhikshuni is not always possible. Not many nuns can afford two plane tickets when they need to travel. In Hong Kong, when I asked a monk who was one of our ordaining masters about this, he advised that we do the best we can. If we cannot find another bhikshuni to accompany us, we should ask a sramanerika; if there is no sramanerika, we should ask a laywoman. The abbess said that these rules were made principally for the safety of young nuns, and perhaps there was not as much danger for older nuns.

Three practices are essential for the bhikshuni sangha: *posadha, varsa,* and *pravarana. Posadha* is the bhikshunis' twice-monthly confession ceremony. Before it begins, all the nuns shave their heads, and then the bhikshunis go upstairs to do the ceremony. It is difficult to express how wonderful it is to be surrounded by many bhikshunis, doing the confession ritual that bhikshunis have done together for twenty-five hundred years, since the time of the Buddha. *Varsa* is the three-month rains retreat held during the summer monsoon, and *pravarana* is the ceremony at its conclusion. It was inspiring to be in an environment where I could do these with other nuns, taking part in traditions that nuns have found valuable for centuries.

PRACTICE AND SUPPORT

Most Chinese nunneries do the Pure Land practice of meditating on Amitabha Buddha, together with some Ch'an (Zen) practice. Others nunneries emphasize Ch'an meditation. The nunneries where I lived are called Lu-zong, or Vinaya School. Here, they learn and practice Vinaya in detail for at least five years before going on to other practices. I also visited a bhikshuni college with a strict course, run by an extremely bright nun at Wu Tai Shan. The women train as novices for two years; then, if they do well, they take the *siksamana* ordination and become a probationary nun. After completing that training, they become bhikshunis. About one hundred sixty nuns were there when I visited, with the college holding three hundred at the maximum. They were packed in rows of nine girls, sleeping on one large platform. Their robes and books were kept near them, but they had nothing else. They just studied and lived simply. It was very impressive.

A Tibetan lama, Khenpo Jigme Phuntsok Rinpoche, had the *Longchen Nyingthik* translated into Chinese, and teaches that, as well as other texts, to thousands of Chinese disciples. Many Chinese monastics want to learn and practice Tibetan Buddhism, but do not want others to know they do so. However, the nuns I knew practiced openly. Several were doing *ngondro*, the preliminary practices of the Tibetan tradition, in Chinese. They did the Vajrasattva hundred-syllable mantra, and one nun had finished one hundred thousand prostrations while others had just begun.

The nuns are not well supported financially. The government does not support the nunneries as far as I know. Although some benefactors offer a generous lunch from time to time, the nuns need to receive money from their families to eat well. Nevertheless, everybody gets the same food, and all the nuns are vegetarian. I stayed at a nunnery in Yangzhou that was very poor because nobody visited the neighborhood where it was located. The government had given these nuns an old, destroyed temple in a park to rebuild. The nuns had no money, so an old nun would sit outside and call to passersby in the park, "It is very meritorious to give generously." Sometimes people would sneer at her, and other times they would give a small amount. Gradually, and with difficulty, the nuns are rebuilding the monastery.

The original nunnery in Guangzhou was built in the seventeenth century. During the Cultural Revolution it was completely destroyed and parts of the site were turned into a factory. Afterwards, when it was returned to the nuns, they had to wait for the lay people inhabiting the building to move out. Some devotees in Hong Kong and a nunnery in Singapore donated money to these nuns, and now, ten years later, their temple, complete with a nuns' college, is almost rebuilt.

GOVERNMENTAL INFLUENCE

During the Cultural Revolution, most monastics in China had to disrobe and return to their families. Our abbess was told to burn her sutras and her robes. Instead, she hid the sutras, in spite of the danger, and slashed her robes, but continued to wear them, telling the officials that she had no other clothes. For many years she had to work in a paper factory and grow her hair long, but she still observed her monastic precepts. She kept a fan to hide her hands when putting them together to show respect for the Buddha. Whenever she offered incense, she put perfume around the room to hide the scent. Still people were suspicious and eventually she was called to attend a political meeting. Apparently the abbess had a special relationship with the bodhisattvas: she prayed to them for help and had a dream in which a giant Buddha put a huge candy in the mouth of the woman who accused her. When the abbess went to the meeting the next day, that woman did not open her mouth! Somehow the nuns survived: they hid; they disguised themselves; they tried to blend in with the environment around them. Their courage, conviction in the Dharma, and strength of character in these difficult circumstances is inspiring. But the minute it was safe, the abbess shaved her head again. She then traveled around Guangzhou to look for other nuns and persuaded them to shave their heads and resume their lives as nuns.

Although the Chinese government presently appears to give religious freedom, there are nonetheless many restrictions and subtle dangers. The government is terrified of anybody who might be a bit different or threaten the society's stability. Government notices of rules it established for the nunneries are posted on the walls. These rules are often unclear and thus difficult to follow properly. At any time government officials can accuse the nuns of breaking them and cause trouble for the nunnery. Although the government allows nunneries to be rebuilt, it limits the number of people who can be ordained, and the monastics have to attend political meetings regularly. Our abbess was called to many time-consuming meetings, but in order to accomplish anything she had to please the authorities by attending them.

Becoming a Bhikshuni

The bhikshuni lineage never took root in Tibet. It was hard for Tibetan women to go to India and difficult for Indian nuns to travel over the Himalayas to Tibet. However, it seems a few bhikshunis lived in Tibet, and records of some bhikshuni ordinations in Tibet were found. People are re-searching this. The bhikshu ordination for monks was almost lost during the time of King Langdarma many centuries ago. Most of the monks were killed or forcefully disrobed, but three who survived fled to Kham, Eastern Tibet. There they met two Chinese monks who completed the required quorum of five monks to give ordination. If Tibetan monks could enlist the aid of Chinese monks, I feel that nuns in the Tibetan tradition should be able to enlist the help of Chinese monks and nuns who now give the bhikshuni ordination.

I feel that becoming a bhikshuni is important for several reasons. First, a central land is defined in the scriptures as a place which has the four classes of Buddhist disciples: bhikshus, bhikshunis, and lay practitioners of both sexes. If a place has no bhikshunis, it is not a central land. Second, why should seventy-year-old nun still be a novice? At the time of the Buddha, the women were not novices forever; they became bhikshunis. Third, hold-ing the bhikshuni ordination changes one in a very deep way. This is my experience and that of other women who have become bhikshunis. We feel more responsible for our practice, for upholding the Dharma, and for the welfare of sentient beings. Our self-respect and self-confidence increase. Therefore, I believe that if one is seriously going to be a nun, at some point she should consider becoming a bhikshuni.

I would like to see bhikshuni ordinations occur in India so that the nuns who cannot afford to go to Hong Kong or Taiwan where the ordination is currently given can attend. In that way, the bhikshuni sangha will return to its land of origin. Some excellent abbesses and Vinaya masters in China and Taiwan could be invited to India to give the ordination. The Tibetan monks could observe the ceremony; or if they would agree, they could perform the bhikshu part of the ordination, because within one day of being ordained by the bhikshuni sangha, a new bhikshuni must be ordained by the bhikshu sangha.

Western Buddhist practitioners can help with cross-cultural contact in the larger Buddhist community. Because many of us have lived in diverse cultures and thus have transcended cultural differences to some extent, we have the possibility to clarify misunderstandings among various Buddhist traditions. For example, many Chinese have seen Tantric iconography and have misconceptions about the Vajrayana. Similarly, many Tibetans have misconceptions about other Buddhist traditions. It is important that as many people as possible meet and converse with those from other Buddhist traditions in their own and other countries. We need to keep an open mind and try to widen the dialogue so that misconceptions can be eliminated.

A Nun in Exile: From Tibet to Mundgod

Sramanerika Thubten Lhatso

*B*orn in the 1930s, Sramanerika *Thubten Lhatso ordained as a nun when she was a child and practiced in her native province of Kham, Tibet, before going to Lhasa. Wanting to practice the Dharma in freedom, she left Chinese-occupied Tibet in the 1980s and went to India. There she was instrumental in establishing Jangchub Choling Nunnery in South India, where she is now one of the senior nuns.*

I WAS BORN IN A VILLAGE IN KHAM, IN THE EASTERN PART OF TIBET, MANY YEARS BEFORE THE CHINESE OCCUPATION OF OUR COUNTRY. The terrain was beautiful, but travel was difficult. Most people were peasants working the land, so we tended to stay close to our birthplace. No nunnery existed near my village in Kham, so I, like some other nuns, did not experience living in a nuns' community while in Tibet. However I would like to share my experience of being a nun in Tibet and now as a refugee in India.

I became a nun when I was twelve years old. In "old Tibet" many families wanted at least one of their children to be a monastic as it was regarded very meritorious for the family. Therefore, since my family had two daughters, my parents said that one of us must become a nun. Since I was not adept at doing work around the house, in the fields, or with the animals, I was the one who ordained. Although I became a nun at a young age, I was unable to receive many teachings as no lama or monastery existed nearby. My father taught me to read and write the Tibetan language, and I stayed at my family's house until I was twenty-one. Tibetan nuns, even those in nunneries, did not do philosophical studies or debate at that time, but mostly engaged in rituals and meditation practices to purify the mind and create positive potential. Thus, during those years, I did many Nyung Ne, the two-day fasting retreat of Chenresig, the Buddha of compassion, as well as chanted one hundred thousand Praises to Tara.

When I was twenty-one, my mother passed away. A lama living in the mountains nearby came to our home at that time to do prayers for my mother and the other villagers. He also gave teachings to the lay people and the seven nuns in the area. He instructed us to do many Nyung Ne practices, which we did, together with one hundred thousand recitations of Chenresig's mantra. We also completed one hundred thousand recitations of the praise to Lama Tsong Khapa, together with guru yoga. Five of us nuns then went to the lama and stayed in retreat where we recited one hundred thousand refuge mantra and did many other recitations and practices. These practices helped us to purify our negative actions, deepen our confidence in the Three Jewels, and develop love and compassion. At age twenty-two, I received the sramanerika vow. I also received the Vajrayogini initiation and did that practice daily, but was unable to do the retreat due to the turbulence caused by the communist occupation of my country.

In 1958, my father, my teacher, and I left for Lhasa, thinking the situation might be better there. However, Lhasa was also occupied by the communist Chinese, and the atmosphere there was extremely tense. Fortunately, I had an audience with His Holiness the Dalai Lama there, which gave me much strength and confidence, qualities that would do me well in what was to come. By the spring of 1959, the Chinese controlled all of Lhasa, and we feared that our old way of life and our religious institutions were in jeopardy. My teacher stayed at Drepung Monastery just outside Lhasa, while we stayed in the city itself. When fighting between the Tibetans and Chinese broke out in March 1959, my father and I wanted to flee that very night. Although we were unable to leave then, my teacher escaped. The following morning my father told me that we must leave that night and instructed me to get our things that were at friend's home. While I was gone, the Chinese captured my father. On my way back, I saw my father standing on the road with the Chinese police. I wanted to go to him and hold him so they could not take him, but I dared not because the Chinese might have killed us both. Helplessly, I watched as they took him away to a destination unknown to me.

Finding my father was difficult because the Kham dialect I spoke was different from the dialect spoken in Lhasa, so I could not easily communicate with people. However, after two months, I succeeded in locating him in one of the prisons. Finally, when some Westerners—I think they were Americans—came to visit Tibet, the Chinese released some of the old prisoners, my father among them. At that time I was living in Lhasa and doing my religious practice. However, the communist Chinese regarded religious practice as useless and religious people as parasites on society, so they ordered me to work. Both my father and I began to work as manual laborers. Since he had to carry soil, sometimes his legs were completely swollen due to the strain. Exhausted from working all day, we were forced to attend political meetings organized by the Chinese communists each evening. During that period, I and many others suffered so much. However, we regarded this as being due to our previous karma. The Buddha said, "Happiness arises from our previous positive actions, and suffering from our negative ones," so we tried not to be angry with those oppressing us. In any case, anger is useless in such situations: it only adds more emotional turmoil to the physical suffering that one is already experiencing. In addition, when angry, we do not think clearly and often make wrong decisions or act brashly, bringing more suffering to ourselves and others.

In 1972, my father passed away. We had been working and waiting in Lhasa, hoping that the Chinese occupation would end soon and that Tibet would regain its independence. That did not happen; but in the early 1980s restrictions relaxed a little, and the Chinese allowed some Tibetans to go to India. I wanted to go to India, but to do so, I needed a letter from a Tibetan there saying that we were relatives and asking me to come for a visit. I sent a letter to one of my teachers at Ganden Monastery in South India, and he sent me a letter of invitation, which I took to the Chinese office in Lhasa to get the papers necessary for travel to India. I told the Chinese officers that he was my relative, not my teacher, and requested to go to India for only three months to see him. When permission to go finally came through, I left all my belongings in Tibet, as if I was planning to return. Had I not done that, they would have suspected me of not intending to return and prevented me from leaving.

Thus I became a refugee. I stayed one month in Nepal and then went to Bodhgaya, India, where I received teachings on the bodhisattvas' practices. Then I went to Drepung Monastery, reconstructed in South India by Tibetans in exile, to see my teacher. After visiting him in Drepung, I went to Dharamsala where I received teachings on the eight texts of the Lamrim, the gradual path to enlightenment. I also had the fortune to receive some initiations and teachings on the bodhisattvas' practice in Varanasi, the Kalachakra initiation in Bodhgaya, and teachings on the Guru Puja as well as various initiations in Dharamsala. Having been unable to receive many teachings as a young nun and having had to do hard manual labor under the Chinese for many years, I was delighted to finally have the opportunity to learn more about the Dharma which I cherished so much.

ESTABLISHING JANGCHUB CHOLING NUNNERY

When I first went to see my teacher in Mundgod, South India, there was not a nunnery there. Later, while Jangchub Choling Nunnery was being constructed, the Tibetan Women's Association told me I was welcome to join the nunnery, but I declined at that time. In January 1987, a representative from the Tibetan Welfare Office invited me to attend the opening ceremony of the nunnery even though I did not intend join it. His Holiness the Dalai Lama was going to be present, and I thought it would be good to receive his blessing, so I went to Mundgod to help with the preparations before his arrival. Since the nunnery had just been completed, it was very dusty and required a lot of cleaning and decorating to make it nice before the opening ceremony. All the nuns in the area—nearly twenty of us—were asked to be present for His Holiness' visit, which we were only too happy to do. Some nuns were very old, coming from the old people's home next door to the nunnery. Others were very young, in their young teens.

While His Holiness was at the nunnery, he asked if anyone was from Tibet. When I replied positively, he said, "There are many monasteries for the monks in India, but very few nunneries. I would like nunneries to be opened in all the big Tibetan settlements in India. Whenever I meet someone who could assist with this, especially those from the Tibetan Women's Association, I ask them to help the nuns. Many Westerners ask me why there are so many monasteries for the monks and hardly any nunneries for the nuns. Now Jangchub Choling Nunnery is opening and I am very happy. Please learn the Dharma well. Since the nunnery is located near both Ganden and Drepung Monasteries, you will not face many problems finding teachers. You must study hard and become expert nuns in the future." After His Holiness had said this, I could not just leave the nuns at Mundgod. As a senior nun, I felt responsible to enact His Holiness' wishes and to care for the development of the young nuns. Since he had emphasized that we must study hard and make the nunnery successful, I decided to stay, join the nunnery, and do what I could to help the nuns. Only a few of the living quarters for the nuns had been completed, and more construction was desperately needed. We had no water or electricity so the sanitation was poor. Due to a shortage of housing at the nunnery, the elder nuns stayed in the old people's home, where their rooms had no doors, windows, or proper bedding. The younger nuns whose families lived nearby slept at their family's house. For almost eleven months, I stayed alone at the nunnery at night while the other nuns lived elsewhere.

In the spring of 1987, the first international meeting of Buddhist women was held in Bodhgaya. Although I did not attend, I learned it was highly successful and led to the establishment of Sakyadhita, the international organization for Buddhist women. Venerable Jampa Tsedroen, one of Geshe Thubten Ngawang's students from the Tibet Center in Germany, attended this conference and afterwards came to our nunnery in Mundgod. She wanted to be with nuns, and in addition, the Department of Religious and Cultural Affairs of the Tibetan government-in-exile asked her to visit

Jangchub Choling. When Jampa Tsedroen asked to stay in the nunnery, we told her that she was most welcome, but we had neither a proper room nor bedding for her. All we had to offer was a hard wooden bed with one bed sheet, so she stayed at Ganden Monastery nearby. The next day she sponsored a Guru Puja, which the nuns performed, and she photographed the nuns and our facilities. She explained that she wanted to find sponsors so that we could build proper rooms, toilets, bathrooms, and kitchen. When the rooms were built, the young nuns came to live at the nunnery.

The Tibetan Welfare Office in our area helped us sponsor the nuns' living costs. They gave forty rupees a month for each young nun who came to study, and each nun had to bring thirty additional rupees from her family in order to cover her expenses. The following year, when Geshe Thubten Ngawang came to the nunnery, we asked for help, and he and Jampa Tsedroen found a sponsor for each nun. The Welfare Office asked Geshe Khenrab Thargye to teach us, and Jampa Tsedroen also requested Geshe Konchog Tsering to instruct the nuns. Both of these excellent *geshes* continue to teach the nuns. Whatever we have now is due to the kindness of all these people.

The Welfare Office, together with another Western nun, provided us with religious texts, English textbooks, and exercise books. All the nuns are most grateful to the Westerners who made it possible for us to build facilities and establish an educational program. Last year, we finished the construction of more living quarters, classrooms, and a dining hall, sponsored by Ms. Baker and many people from the West. Westerners have helped not only our nunnery, but many Tibetan institutions—nunneries, monasteries, hospitals, and schools, and we are grateful for this. What we Tibetans have been able to accomplish in exile is also due to the kindness of His Holiness the Dalai Lama. Countless bodhisattvas have appeared on earth, but they have not been able to subdue our minds. Even now His Holiness is trying to subdue us and show us the way to enlightenment, so we are very lucky.

Daily Life in the Nunnery

As for our daily schedule: we get up at 5:00 A.M. and go to the temple for our morning prayers, after which we dedicate the positive potential for the peace and happiness of all sentient beings and the long life of His Holiness the Dalai Lama. After breakfast, we attend teachings for one or two hours. This is followed by debate, which allows us to discuss and reach a clearer understanding of the Buddha's teachings. Only in recent years have nuns begun to study the philosophical texts and debate their meanings, activities in which previously only monks engaged. This advancement in nuns' education has occurred due to His Holiness' instructions and the interest of the young nuns. Lunch follows, and in the afternoon we have Tibetan and English classes. In the evenings, we again do prayers in the main temple for an hour. We principally do Tara Puja, as well as other practices. After that, we again have debate, after which the nuns study on their own, reading books and memorizing the scriptures. We go to bed around midnight.

In general, the nuns cooperate well with each other and with those in positions of responsibility in the nunnery. Since I am the most senior nun, I have to discipline and advise them when necessary. They follow my counsel and are not rebellious or headstrong. Sometimes I have had to hit some of the younger ones when they misbehaved, but they don't mind it too much. They do not take it seriously or fight against me, as they know that my intentions are to help them be good nuns. In fact, when I told them that a few other nuns and I were going to *Life as a Western Buddhist Nun*, many of them cried and said they couldn't enjoy the Tibetan New Year's celebrations because the senior nuns would be away!

On Mondays, we have a day off, but I do not allow the nuns to be idle then. They must study or memorize on those days too. Even at New Year's they don't have special holidays. Every now and again they do ask for a holiday, and this is fine. Although it is difficult to establish a nunnery from scratch with few resources, I think we have done quite well. I am very happy that the nuns now have better educational opportunities than in the past, and that many of them are taking advantage of this. In 1995, nuns from the various nunneries in exile had a large debate session, lasting many days in Dharamsala. At the conclusion, for the first time in history, some of the best nuns debated at the main temple, in front of His Holiness the Dalai Lama. Of course, some were nervous, but afterwards many people commented how well they did. I continuously request them to study and practice well for the sake of sentient beings and to pray for the long of life of His Holiness and our other teachers. We are so fortunate to have this opportunity to learn and practice the Buddha's teachings!

A Strong Tradition Adapting to Change: The Nuns in Korea

Chi-Kwang Sunim

Having grown up in Australia, Chi-Kwang Sunim ordained as a bhikshuni in Korea, where she studied and practiced for many years. She currently travels between Lotus Lantern International Buddhist Center in Korea and Australia, where she is establishing a monastery.

AS A WESTERN BUDDHIST NUN, I FEEL VERY FORTUNATE TO HAVE LIVED IN KOREA AND TRAINED IN THIS TRADITION FOR MANY YEARS. Having hundreds of years experience, the Korean bhikshunis have established a systematic, effective way of training new nuns. They begin with a novice period, progress to sutra study schools, and go on to meditation halls or other vocations of their choosing. The monastic life here is inspiring, although, as in other Asian countries, it is undergoing change due to the country's modernization and developments in the predominant Chogye Order.

To understand Korean Buddhism and monastic life, it is helpful to remember that many influences, spanning over a thousand years, have brought Buddhism to where it is today. These include five hundred years of Confusion law, as well as Taoism, shamanism, and animism, which are still practiced in many temples. In recent years, Christianity also has influenced some city temples, which now have choirs, Sunday schools, and Christian-style religious services. Over time, Korean Buddhism and Korean nuns have absorbed these influences and evolved with their own unique flavor.

The nuns' communities are independent from the monks', although sometimes they reside on the same mountain. However, the monks and nuns may attend formal ceremonies, communal events, Dharma talks, ordination ceremonies, and funerals together at a large temple. From time to time abbots and abbesses come together for annual training periods and discussion of the events at their temples. Apart from these instances of sharing, the nuns live separate, self-sufficient lives, with their own supporters, training schools and meditation halls, in thousands of temples varying in size from small hermitages to very large temples. They even have their own bhikshuni masters and "family" lineages. In the latter, disciples of the same master are "sisters," nuns who are colleagues of their teacher are "aunts," and so on.

The monks and nuns have similar life styles, temple organizations, robes, sutra schools, and meditation halls, although the nuns' four-year sutra schools are more developed than those of the monks. Because of this, the monks generally show respect for the nuns, especially those who are elder or positions senior to their own. The nuns also have a very strong meditation order, where in over thirty-five bhikshuni meditation halls, twelve hundred or more nuns practice meditation almost continuously throughout the year.

The lineage of Korean bhikshunis is not completely clear. Recently while staying in Chon Yong Sa temple in Seoul, I discovered its old history log listing the unbroken lineage of abbesses. Queen Son Tok founded the temple 1,350 years ago, when she, her family, and servants became bhikshunis and resided here. Also, in Chong Yarng Sa Temple in Seoul, an unbroken lineage of bhikshunis continues to this day. Records in Buddhist libraries reveal descriptions of early ordinations even prior to this period and tell of the transmission of the Korean bhikshuni ordination to Japanese nuns. Many stories, too, have been passed down about various queens, many of whom became bhikshunis, and their great works to support the Dharma. It is suspected that although the bhikshuni order did not die out during the Confucian rule or the Japanese occupation, the ordination procedures for both monks and nuns were simplified.

Older nuns speak of their teachers and their teachers' lineage, and some nuns in the last fifty years have been considered great masters, although little is written about their teachings or lives. One great bhikshuni told me, "If ever you become enlightened, don't let anyone know, because you will have to spend the rest of your life having to prove it." We are often told not to discuss our practice too much, but to let it blossom in our clear and compassionate actions. We should confide only in a trustworthy teacher who can guide our practice and actions, so that we are not caught in thoughts and experiences even of enlightenment. However, this makes me wonder if nuns throughout history have not been written about due to their silence and humility!

Nowadays, the most senior bhikshunis are generally well known. They preside over the main rituals and ordinations and are the masters of their lineages or heads of major temples, sutra schools, or meditation halls. Sometimes they are simply known for being a devout, dedicated bhikshuni and may or may not have exceptional abilities. Not all of the senior bhikshunis have many disciples, but they usually are part of a large "family" lineage, with many younger nuns following in their footsteps. The products of their work are found in the temples, sutra schools, and meditation halls they have constructed, as well as in their Dharma teaching, translation work, and the role model of monastic life they set.

The Training of a Novice

The training of a novice takes from six months to one year. During this time a woman is not yet a nun. Her head is not shaven—although her hair is cut short—and she may leave the temple at any time. In this period, she has the opportunity to choose her teacher, though often she will do this shortly before she ordains. However, some women come with knowledge of or commitment to a teacher in this or another temple. During these first six months, her training is not in the hands of her teacher, but in those of the kitchen supervisor or other senior nuns who guide her through her novice period. She works in the kitchen, serves the nuns in her temple, and becomes familiar with monastic life. After she has learned the basic chanting and monastic deportment and has undergone long periods of bowing and repentance daily, she is tested for about one month. She needs to have a health certificate and is checked for physical ailments. In addition, her personal history is examined; if there is any major flaw in it, she may not become a nun of the Chogye Order. After completing this examination, she receives the sramanerika ordination and returns to her teacher, where she spends another year.

During this next year, she serves her teacher and prepares for the examination to enter a sutra school, for which she needs to know some Chinese characters and to memorize basic texts such as *Admonitions to Beginning Students*. Written twelve hundred years ago by Master Chinul (Bojo-kuksa), it teaches both monks and nuns the discipline of a newly ordained monastic: how to walk, act, and speak with others; the importance of respecting one's seniors and helping one's juniors; and so on. Once she has learned to live by this basic standard, she begins to study other sutras and prepares to enter a monastic training college.

SUTRA SCHOOLS

Both monks and nuns have established colleges where the ordained train and study. I spent only one year in Un Mun Sa temple, where my teacher, Myong Song Sunim, has been the abbess and senior lecturer for twenty years. Here I experienced the complex, yet inspiring community life of 250 nuns. Only five major sutra schools, with 150 to 250 nuns each, exist in Korea, although there are several smaller ones. If a nun does not get into one of the main sutra schools, where it is difficult to be accepted, she can go to a smaller sutra school or try to enter a year later, after receiving further training from her teacher. The first year students vary in age from twenty to forty-five. Some nuns may stay for several years with their teacher before going to the sutra school, and some older nuns may bypass the sutra school and go directly to a meditation hall.

Training in the sutra schools is rigorous. The students eat, sleep, and study in one room. Their main teacher lectures about three hours a day, with the nuns following the text in Chinese characters, which requires several hours of preparation. Special Dharma lectures are given weekly by visiting teachers, along with various other teachings in the arts, languages, and music. In addition, a work period is scheduled for two or three hours a day, during which the nuns look after the vegetable gardens; harvest, pickle, dry, and store food; or cook for the community. The nuns in the final year at the sutra schools are in positions of authority and lead the younger nuns. Several will hold yearly, demanding positions such as assistant treasurer, head cook, or office worker.

The diet is vegetarian, simple yet nourishing, and often served attractively. Senior nuns are offered a slightly different diet, which is less hot and salty, and the sick are given special food as required. Meals are eaten formally, with chanting before and after the meal.

The nuns also do work that directly contributes to society, with each nun selecting a yearly project. Some work in orphanages, old people's homes, hospitals, or answer calls on the telephone hotline, while others produce newsletters, and Dharma books, and pamphlets. A few nuns work at Buddhist radio, broadcasting daily Buddhist news, music, chanting, and Dharma talks. Other nuns work in Sunday schools and summer retreats for children, or take children from orphanages or the elderly from old peoples' homes on outings. The nuns involved in each project raise the funds to do their work.

Although these sutra training schools are considered Buddhist universities in terms of their scholarship, they are more than this. The nuns learn to be wholesome, generous people, qualities often lacking in society. They learn not only how to wear their robes, how to eat, and so forth, but also how to communicate with others. In short, they learn how to be satisfied and happy as nuns. It is not possible to isolate oneself, for the nuns constantly have to interact with each other in community life. Sometimes their interactions are painful, but through these experiences, the nuns know they will become more understanding of others. The nuns go from being very immature people, with lots of fears and unrealistic ideas about monastic life, to becoming more open, accepting, and willing to listen and engage with others. They develop commitment to the community as a whole, and one can see in their faces compassion and wisdom taking shape. Some of these nuns become outstanding teachers or leaders.

Sufficient time for meditation is lacking in the sutra schools. The nuns attend morning, midday, and evening services in the main Buddha Hall. Doing a variety of communal activities, they learn to be mindful even without long hours of meditation. Hours of chanting and studying the Buddha's teachings helps to calm and deepen the mind; yet I believe more meditation would increase their clarity in daily life. The sutra school I attended had an hour for meditation in the daily schedule, but only a few nuns came. When they are young and busy, they do not appreciate the value of this practice. Nor are they introduced to it properly, although they read a lot about it. Thus, even a graduate from a Buddhist university may not have learned how to meditate well. This is quite unfortunate, yet common. However, a nun may do chanting or other practices which purify her mind, and by disciplining herself, she may become a good practitioner.

The nuns also have to serve the elder nuns and their teachers. By providing whatever their teachers request or require, the nuns develop a caring attitude toward others. They appreciate this learning situation, which helps them to develop respect and compassion and to diminish arrogance and stubbornness. Upon occasion tempers are short and people abruptly correct each other, but the nuns learn to tolerate such behavior. I have not often seen major disputes although I have seen nuns misbehave. In that case, they are brought before the assembly of nuns, where they must repent or at least explain their behavior. They are cautioned or even reprimanded, but this is generally done out of kindness and not in a hurtful way.

I have seen nuns demonstrate against the elders' opinions. The individuality of the young nuns and weakening discipline contribute to this development in recent years. As communities have grown, it is difficult for a few teachers to control large numbers of students. On one occasion some years back, the students demonstrated against the abbess and her staff. This provoked concerns about how sutra schools should be run in order to prevent such situations from getting out of hand. At such times elders from other communities intervene, giving advice and strength.

BHIKSHUNI ORDINATION

After four years of training in Vinaya and preparing for bhikshuni ordination, a nun will graduate from sutra school and will take bhikshuni ordination. With more women ordaining and remaining monastics than men, the female sangha is strong in Korea. This strengthening of nuns seems somehow to threaten the monks, so to control the situation, subtle but constant restrictions are being placed on the bhikshunis. Within the Chogye Order, the bhikshunis have created with their own funding, a sub-order of senior nuns whose job is to be aware of major problems and rifts in the nuns' sangha, to resolve issues quickly, and to work in harmony with the other branches of the order. However, bhikshunis hold no major positions in the headquarters of the Chogye Order and are unable to lecture there as in the past. They rely on good relations with senior monks for their voice to be heard. Although some nuns have studied Vinaya extensively, they have not yet made a graduate school for Vinaya studies as the monk have. Since this contributes to the monks being more severe with the nuns, it would be wise for the nuns to improve their Vinaya education.

Temple rules and monastic guidelines are emphasized in addition to the Vinaya. In the meditation halls or the sutra schools in Korea, the monks and nuns do not break any major rules and seldom transgress even the minor ones. Within the community, they live very carefully. However, as the country and temples become stronger and wealthier, corruption on some levels is inevitable. More Korean monks and nuns travel abroad and reports of their conduct have not always been positive. As a visitor in another country, one does not always act as one does at home.

When I first arrived in Korea many years ago, the temples were extremely poor. We needed to work every day simply to have enough to eat, and we valued and shared the few clothes we had. We also cherished our meditation time very much. Because monastics cared about community life and respected their teachers and the sangha, rules were not frequently broken. When a monastic becomes more concerned with securing his or her comfort or position, carelessness, greed, and fear more easily arise.

MEDITATION HALLS

During meditation seasons, the discipline in the meditation halls is very strong. As in all Korean temples, those in the meditation halls get up very early, usually about 2:00 or 3:00 A.M. Until they go to bed, which may be 10:00 or 11:00 P.M., they have minimal personal time. They meditate for ten to fourteen hours a day and the atmosphere is light and joyous.

After finishing sutra school, a nun may choose life in the meditation hall. About a quarter of those attending sutra school go on to become meditation nuns after they graduate. Most nuns choose to live in a small temple with their teacher, become abbess in their own temples, or take graduate courses at a major Buddhist university. A few choose social work or other professional areas but these too need further studies at a university.

In Korea, there are at least ten large meditation halls, each having fifty to one hundred nuns, and about fifteen medium meditation halls having ten to thirty nuns. There are also many small gatherings with just a few nuns meditating together. Often located in beautiful areas, the meditation halls may be part of a large nuns' temple or near a large monks' temple. If so, the hall is in a quiet area away from visitors and tourists. There are two major meditation seasons—in the summer and the winter—each lasting three months, and in the spring and autumn there are two-month "off-season" retreats. Most large meditation halls are open year round and the most serious practitioners stay and practice continuously there. In some temples, nuns undertake retreats for three years or more and are not allowed to leave the temple under any circumstances during that time, unless they are very sick.

In the meditation hall nuns alternate sitting for fifty minutes and walking for ten minutes, with three-hour sessions before dawn, in the morning, afternoon, and evening. The basic discipline of the meditation hall is decided at a meeting at the beginning of the retreat. At this time, the meditation hall nuns also choose who will be the leader of the hall and assign other work positions that keep the temple functioning well. In the past we had to cook and heat the rooms by making fires, but now electricity and modern conveniences have taken over these difficult chores in many temples.

The nuns sit in order of seniority, according to the number of years they have been ordained. The head of the meditation hall is in charge of training the younger nuns. If a younger nun has a problem with her meditation, she goes to this nun, who either helps her or takes her to see a master. Almost all the meditation halls are affiliated with a main temple where there is a master. At the beginning of the meditation season, and once every two weeks, the nuns attend a talk by this master or listen to a taped talk if they are unable to go. If the main temple is far away, they hear a Dharma talk only a few times during the meditation season, and the elder nuns take over the responsibility of guiding the younger nuns in the meantime.

The day before a lecture, the nuns bathe and look after their personal needs. They do whatever chores need to be done and sometimes relax or go for a walk in the mountains. After listening to the Dharma talk the following day, they continue with the meditation schedule. The days go by very quickly, and one finds that four or five hours of sleep is sufficient. If drowsiness occurs in meditation, one corrects her posture and continues to practice diligently. Along with meditation practice, some nuns may chant or bow as repentance practice during break times. They often do some exercise, T'ai Chi or yoga, but generally this is not a communal function.

The cushions in the hall are laid out very close to one another, with the nuns facing the wall when meditating. They do a koan practice. Here a nun receives a koan from a master and works with it throughout her life. This differs from Japanese Zen, where one goes through a series of koans which open to many aspects of the one. In Korea they work with the one which will open to many aspects of the others. A nun's mind should not become attached to the words or the storyline of the koan. In this way, she comes to the essence. Some teachers give the koan, "What is it?" or "What is this?" In other words, "What is this mind? What is this thing we call I or me?" A story accompanies each koan, and hopefully one is left with a puzzle or a deeper sense of doubt about this question. If practice is very strong, one goes beyond the words and is left with a very curious, open, aware sense of inquiry from moment to moment. If inquiry into the koan is not alive, one often finds that one is dreaming, deluded, or lethargic. A person who is not interested in diligent practice will not last very long in the meditation halls, but one who has practiced a long time has this very "alive word." The question becomes a doubt or sensation of curious unknowing, and one is completely absorbed in this present moment. Serious practitioners have a certain joy and strength that pervades them, and others' problems seem to dissolve in their presence. At the least, these practitioners show us how to work with and resolve problems.

Some practitioners in Korea now do other practices: *vipassana* they learned from Southeast Asian monks or Tantra learned from Tibetans. From my observation, providing that one does not disturb others or expect them to follow, it is acceptable to engage in other practices. Such practitioners are usually quiet about their practice.

There is a certain uniformity and consistency among the nuns in the meditation hall. Of course the nuns are individuals, but they perform their duties quietly and contentedly without drawing attention to themselves. The junior nuns are quickly reprimanded if they stand out and are taught how to live amicably within the hall. If a nun is sick, she may go to the infirmary, and if her posture is painful, she can change her position. But because one sits for long periods, movement within the meditation session naturally becomes less and less.

The hall has a sense of lightness, humor, and joy. Each day the nuns share tea and talk together. The senior nuns talk about the masters and great nuns they knew, thus informally giving teachings and guidance on how to practice. Having tea together is an important part of the practice, and young nuns who do not want to attend are reprimanded. Unless one is old or sick, she is expected to share in all activities, even social times. Once a season a week of non-sleep practice occurs. During this week every effort is exerted to sit upright and concentrate on one's koan. A long thin stick is gently tapped on the shoulders of a dozing nun with a cracking sound that alerts the whole room. The days and nights pass, but not without great effort and suffering to stay alert. However, as thoughts and dreams diminish, the mind becomes clear and lucid. On the last morning, the nuns trek in the mountains to get some exercise before resting.

At the end of the season, the nuns are free to continue sitting in the meditation hall or they may travel to other meditation temples. Although the atmosphere may differ depending on whether a hall is close to the city or in magnificent mountain scenery, the meditation halls are generally run in the same way, so the nuns have little difficulty going from one to another.

Close relationships are not encouraged within nuns' communities, and if two nuns are seen together for a long period of time, they are encouraged to separate and will not be accepted in a meditation hall at the same time. Financial support of the meditation nuns is minimal. They receive food and lodging for the three months and a small amount of money when they leave to cover their fare to another temple. Unlike the monks, they are not well supported financially, and very few of the meditation nuns have much money. Their clothes are often old and patched, and they have few possessions. All of the nuns support each other well, giving freely if they have something that someone else needs.

Not all nuns enter a meditation hall after completing sutra school. Some enter a graduate program in Buddhist studies or social work at a university. A few nuns study secular subjects to become doctors, lawyers, artists, or performers. Others are involved in the Buddhist radio and television, which have become very popular recently. One nun has become a famous radio announcer with a popular rating and raises funds for social projects in the community. The working monastics usually live alone or with one other monastic and are not very adept in communal life. Few have ever lived in meditation halls, although many have completed sutra study schools. However, because they have missed out on the nuns' communal life, their monastic quality is lacking. In one way, this is a pity, because in my eyes the monastic communities are the greatest attribute of the Korean monastic life style.

A nun is sometimes expected to hold a position in a temple: abbess, administrator, secretary, director, treasurer, or head of the kitchen. Usually nuns are persuaded to take on these difficult positions due to their seniority, abilities, or popularity. Rarely do they choose to be an administration monastic, as it requires time and effort in areas that are not so conducive to practice and peace of mind. Of course, a mature person will use this opportunity to strengthen and deepen her path. On completion of her duty, she happily returns to the meditation hall or to her home temple to continue her practice.

INSPIRATIONS AND INFLUENCES

I had the opportunity to meet a 102-year-old nun who had meditated for years. She sat bolt upright, with a rosary of black beads and a rosary of white beads twirling together in her left hand. With soundless lips that constantly moved, she silently repeated her mantra. Her eyes gently opened and rested in space in front of her, glistening with the brilliance of awareness. My presence created little movement, other than her right hand grabbing my left firmly and pulling me close to her. When I yelled in her hard-of-hearing ear, "I'm a foreigner," she held up the mingled black and white beads and said, "Lets practice together." When I asked about her past she said, "What past?" and her rosary rolled on as she looked straight at me as if seeing something deep inside. "Lets become enlightened together," she grinned. There was nothing further to be said; I was glued to the cushion, gripped by her hand and her immensity of being.

One of her disciples told me this nun's story. She came to this site after a life in meditation halls. Living in a hut, she kept up her practice as if in a meditation hall. Then another nun appeared who wanted to rebuild the temple. While this nun raised funds and built building after building, the old nun continued to sit eight hours a day. Up until she was ninety-two years old, she still washed her clothes, cleaned her room, and sat. When the number of disciples increased and the workload eased, they persuaded her to let them do her chores. Meanwhile, she continued her practices of sitting and walking meditation. I heard that shortly before she passed on, she said she felt totally free. All that needed to be done was completed and her heart was at peace. She passed away sitting upright, rolling her black and white beads.

There are many nuns like this, who have sat many years in the meditation hall and continue to practice on their own, unknown. A monk like this would have become a great master with thousands flocking to see him. But the nuns prefer to be unknown to the public; they are known only to other meditating nuns and are often forgotten when they retire to live as a hermit. Rarely are bhikshunis elevated to the monks' standard of master, but I have never met a nun who sought this. A few nuns who are apt teachers are not of the Chogye Order. Many propagate the Dharma overseas and have large communities. One even has a community of monks under her, which is a rare occurrence.

Some aspects of the nuns' life in Korea I feel will be detrimental to the bhikshuni order if not looked into carefully. Over the last ten years, many aspects of traditional Korean society have changed, and the attitude of the newly ordained is very different from before. Now many young women are disillusioned with the government and their teachers and reject "the system." Someone entering monastic life with this motivation usually has a hard time because she finds more structure and hierarchy in the temples, sutra schools, and meditation halls. Many young nuns now have strong opinions when they enter the order, and the gap between the old school and new is widening. Elders worry how to discipline the young, and the young are resistant. I do not believe that letting go of discipline so that one acts like a laywoman but calls oneself a nun is correct. Finding a middle ground is not easy, and elders must be sincere, open, present, and practice what they preach. Westernization and technology are not the problem; what we do with them is. If comfort and luxury is what one seeks, being a nun will be very frustrating, for one can never obtain enough external things. We cannot stop changes in society, but throughout history, Buddhist practitioners have continuously developed and communicated what is true and valuable to the human heart. The Buddha's path to true freedom and peace gives us genuine wealth and satisfaction.

SOMETHING ABOUT ZEN

Mitra Bishop Sensei

Joseph Sorrentino

American by birth, Mitra Bishop Sensei received a B.A. from Indiana University, raised two children, and worked in graphic, interior, and architectural design for many years. She first encountered Buddhism while living in Asia. She was ordained at the Rochester Zen Center, where She lived for many years before going to Sogen-ji in Japan to practice under the guidance of the Zen master, Harada Shodo Roshi. She currently lives in New Mexico, where she has founded Mountain Gate Zen Center.

Sentient beings are numberless; I vow to liberate them.
Desires are inexhaustible; I vow to put an end to them.
The Dharmas are boundless; I vow to master them.
The Buddha's Way is unsurpassable; I vow to become it.

THESE VOWS ARE REPEATED DAILY IN ZEN TEMPLES AND MONASTERIES THROUGHOUT THE WORLD. Reminding us of our intention when we practice, they are basic to our school and to Buddhism. "Zen" is the Japanese pronunciation of the Chinese word "Ch'an," which came from the Sanskrit word "*dhyana*," meaning meditation. Meditation is the emphasis of Zen, the core of our meditation practice being *sesshin*, a meditation retreat, which usually lasts a week. In the Rochester Zen Center in New York, and in Sogen-ji, the temple where I lived in Japan, we have these retreats each month. In addition, at Sogen-ji we have two in December: the traditional eight-day Rohatsu Sesshin, celebrating the Buddha's enlightenment, and a follow-up seven-day sesshin.

Centuries ago Zen divided into the Soto Sect and the Rinzai Sect, based on the specific emphases of particular masters. The Rinzai Sect traces its lineage to the Buddha through Lin Chi (Rinzai), a Chinese master famous for his strong, dynamic way of teaching. The Soto style is gentler and puts more emphasis on form. The Rochester Zen Center, although technically a Soto center, is an amalgam of both, as the two main teachers of its founder, Roshi Kapleau, trained in both sects. Sogen-ji's lineage is Rinzai.

In the Rinzai Sect and Rochester's version of Soto, the primary advanced study is koan work. Certain koans have become familiar in the West. Breakthrough koans are those which one works on for years until gaining some degree of understanding. That understanding is broadened and deepened through work on subsequent koans. One of the most famous breakthrough koans is, "What is the sound of one hand clapping?" It has an answer, but not one that can be talked about with one's teacher. Koan work must be experiential; deep meditation is required to solve these koans.

Such intensive meditation is done primarily, though not exclusively, in sesshin. During a Sogen-ji sesshin, we begin the day at 3:30 A.M. with sutra chanting for an hour. After that we go to the zendo (meditation hall) for zazen (meditation) until breakfast. During that early morning meditation period, we also have sanzen (dokusan), a brief, private, one-on-one meeting with our teacher. Our teacher checks our practice, gives us spiritual instruction, and urges us on. When we live in a monastery, temple, or center and work directly with a teacher, we have such private meetings frequently. This is part of the Zen way, and it is very effective in deepening our practice. After breakfast we do chores for a short time and then return to the meditation hall to continue zazen until lunchtime. Following that is rest period, then teisho (Dharma talk) by the teacher, more zazen, a short exercise period, and a light supper. After another short break, we do more formal zazen for a few hours until we retire around 10:30 P.M.

ZEN TRAINING

The emphasis in Zen is on coming to awakening, deepening that awakening to profound levels, and living our lives with that understanding. Accordingly, we place somewhat less emphasis on the precepts than do those schools that focus Vinaya study. We do not ignore the precepts by any means. They are a fundamental basis of practice, for practicing with a confused mind is difficult, and following precepts gives us clarity and simplifies our life, enabling us to meditate deeply.

In Japanese Zen we move as a group from one building to another, marching in file according to seniority, based on one's date of arrival at the temple and whether or not one is ordained—not on how long one has been training. Seniority is a serious aspect of the training in Japanese temples: the bottom line is that if someone more senior asks one to do something, one does it.

We have two training periods a year at Sogen-ji. One is from February 4 to August 4, and the other from August 4 to February 4. So essentially we are in training all the time. Kotai, meaning change, occurs on August 4 and February 4. At this time, the jobs in the temple are rotated, as are our rooms. During each *kotai* the women move clockwise one room around the women's quarters, and our roommates usually change as well. Learning to work with change is a fundamental aspect of our practice of Zen, the idea being to be like water, which can flow with the circumstances. Almost nobody knows until the day of *kotai* who is going to do what job for the next term. There is a very short time in which the people formerly holding jobs can meet with the people newly assigned to them, so that the latter have to scramble to understand their new jobs before they have to do something in their new capacity a few minutes later. At the same time, everyone rushes to move her belongings to her new room, which means the previous occupant has to leave that room first. It's like a grand game of musical chairs!

Sogen-ji is a double monastery, which means both men and women train there. This is relatively unique in Japan, where usually there are either monasteries or nunneries. At Sogen-ji everyone lives the monastic form whether or not they are ordained. It is called a temple as well as a monastery, while the Rochester Zen Center is a "daily practice center," an American term encompassing ordained and lay practice. In the United States, "monk," "nun," and "priest" have different meanings in different temples. In my home temple, the Rochester Zen Center, I was ordained as a priest, which means I can conduct certain ceremonies and run a temple. According to the Japanese system, a priest can also marry although I am not and do not wish to be. "Monk" is used for both men and women in some temples. There are no differences in precepts in my lineage whether one is called a monk, nun, or priest. The titles "*roshi*" and "*sensei*" pertain to one's status as a teacher, and not to one's ordination. Many people practicing Zen in Japan are foreigners, while few Japanese are interested in religious practice these days. In the nineteenth century the Japanese government declared that Buddhist monks and nuns could marry, and that took the teeth out of spiritual practice in many cases. It also hastened the decline of Buddhism in Japan, a trend which unfortunately continues to this day. There are "accredited" temples in Japan where anyone whose parent is a temple priest can study for six months to three years and receive a certificate allowing him to inherit his parent's temple and to conduct ceremonies—usually funerals—to earn a living.

A few serious training temples still exist in Japan, of which Sogen-ji is one. We are fortunate not to be a priest-accrediting temple, so we are not thronged by people who are interested only in getting that certificate. The people who come to Sogen-ji are serious about practice, and if they are not, they leave very quickly because it is a strenuous lifestyle.

The word "sangha" is used in a broad sense both in Rochester and at Sogen-ji and does not refer to ordained people alone. Because so many lay practitioners are serious, it is more difficult to distinguish those of us who are ordained—who have made formal life-long commitments—and those who have families and regular jobs in society yet still meditate regularly each day and spend their vacation time in *sesshin*. Lay practice is strong in America and in Europe and is one of the directions in which Buddhism seems to be going in the West.

Still, a number of us are called to dedicate our entire lives to this practice. In my lineage this means that when we work, we work for the Dharma and not for money. We can be supported for our work, but it cannot be, for example, architecture, engineering, secretarial work, or computer work. Although being a hospice worker would be acceptable, in general most ways that people earn money are not available to us. This is an exercise in faith. As long as we remain in the temple in Japan—which has been in existence for three hundred years and has a strong base of support—we are supported. Our basic needs are taken care of through donations to the temple. In Rochester it is similar. Outside of these temples, however, we are on our own.

The liturgy or the sutra chanting in Sogen-ji and in Rochester is done in both English and Japanese. Our teacher, Harada Shodo Roshi, is very unusual for a Japanese. The only reason we chant in Japanese at all is because the temple is in Japan. Lay supporters come sometimes, and Japanese monks still live at the temple. Otherwise, he would have us do the liturgy in English, the main language in the temple after Japanese. Our teacher is intent on translating all the chants into the languages of the people coming to train, so that they can chant in their own language. He feels that if we hear teachings in our own language they register more, and this is true. If someone staying at Sogen-ji does not speak Japanese, a Western woman who has learned Japanese well over the years is happy to translate when needed. Although Harada Shodo Roshi knows quite a bit of English, the subtle kind of work that one has to do in the private meetings with him requires a translator.

THE PRECEPTS

Every year at the Rochester Zen Center three receiving the precepts ceremonies (*jukai*) for adults and two for children take place. One is held at Thanksgiving, because over the years Thanksgiving has been transformed into a Buddhist holiday in our Zen centers. We also hold *jukai* at New Years, and in the springtime at Vesak, the celebration of the Buddha's birthday.

We take the sixteen bodhisattva precepts. The first three are called the three general resolutions. They are 1) to avoid evil, 2) to do good, and 3) to liberate all sentient beings. These three cover the full range of actions and are a tough order to follow. The next three precepts are the three refuges, formulated as a vow. They are: "I take refuge in Buddha and resolve that, with all beings, I will understand the Great Way whereby the Buddha seed may forever thrive. I take refuge in Dharma and resolve that, with all beings, I will enter deeply into the sutra treasure, whereby my wisdom may grow as vast as the ocean. I take refuge in Sangha and in their wisdom, example, and never-failing help, and resolve to live in harmony with all beings." The final ten precepts are the ten cardinal precepts. Over the years in Rochester we have worked refining the translation of these precepts. They are each put forth as a two-faceted precept, with something to refrain from and something to enhance. They are:

1. Not to kill, but to cherish all life
2. Not to take what is not freely given, but to respect all things
3. Not to lie, but to speak the truth
4. Not to engage in improper sexuality, but to live a life of purity and self-restraint (How this precept is kept depends on one's life circumstances)
5. Not to take substances that confuse the mind, but to keep the mind clear at all times (It is worded in this way because so many things besides liquor can confuse the mind)
6. Not to speak of the misdeeds of others, but to be understanding and sympathetic
7. Not to praise oneself and disparage others, but to work on one's own shortcomings
8. Not to withhold spiritual or material aid, but to give them freely where needed
9. Not to indulge in anger, but to exercise restraint
10. Not to revile the Three Treasures of Buddha, Dharma, and Sangha, but to cherish and uphold them

In addition to our precept-taking ceremonies and repentance and confession ceremonies, we work on these precepts in our formal practice by using a long series of koans. Because the precepts are so profound and can be seen in many ways and at many levels, more than fifty koans are dedicated to precept work, and it takes quite awhile to get through them. The precepts are examined from many different perspectives, beginning with the literal interpretation, proceeding through the Mahayana understanding, and so on all the way to their ultimate nature. In this way, we discover multiple layers of understanding about each precept. To speak on the precepts at all is difficult, because they are much more profound than words can express. As soon as we say one thing, another can also be said that comes at an angle to it and is correct at a certain level.

Because we are still limited beings, we make mistakes and transgress our precepts. To purify and restore our precepts, we do a confession and repentance ceremony before each *sesshin*, before each precept-taking ceremony, and at other times as well. This ceremony has become a basis of serious, deep practice in Rochester. Lay people are included in it, unlike the custom in the strictly monastic traditions in Southeast Asia, Tibet, and China. It has taken Westerners some years to grasp the spirit of these ceremonies. Early on our understanding was rather superficial, so many people attended only because it was required. However, we have been transformed by Dharma talks and practice, so now these confession and repentance ceremonies have become deep and moving. We come out of them feeling cleansed and inspired by people's struggles to keep the precepts. In Rochester, our confession and repentance ceremony is based on the writings of Dogen, the Japanese master who brought the Soto lineage from China. Before the ceremony begins, the leader, who is a senior ordained person, talks about the purpose of repentance and the spirit of the ceremony. The ceremony opens with chanting and a moment of silence. The leader then recites a piece that speaks of openly confessing before the Buddhas and ancestors in order to purify ourselves. After this, a stick of incense is lit and placed in a small incense pot, which is passed from person to person. If we have nothing to confess in that particular ceremony—which rarely happens—we offer the incense pot for a moment and then pass it on. If we have something to confess, we do so. The confession has two parts: revealing our wrongdoings and resolving not to continue those habitual patterns of behavior in the future. When we finish our confession, other people may bring up faults or wrong actions they have observed in us. If nothing is brought up, we pass the incense pot to the next person. The core of the ceremony is the repentance *gatha*, "All evil actions I have committed since time immemorial, stemming from greed, anger, and ignorance, arising from body, speech, and mind, I now repent having committed." It is done nine times toward the end of the ceremony just to cover whatever we might have missed in our specific confession. Revealing our mistakes in this way is very helpful for lightening the heart and effecting change within us.

The Ordination Ceremony

It takes a long time before one is permitted to be ordained in the Zen tradition, although in Japan exceptions are made in the case of children expected to inherit a parent's temple. Various levels of ordination exist. Especially in the Soto Sect, lay people traditionally take the receiving the precepts ceremony as a personal and public commitment to Buddhist practice. At this lay ordination one takes the sixteen bodhisattva precepts and receives a lay *rakusu* (miniature Buddha's robe) and a lay Buddhist name. Zen Buddhist monks, nuns, and priests also take the sixteen bodhisattva precepts. However, while lay people keep them within the context of a householder's lifestyle, fully ordained people are expected to exemplify them as fully as possible for the rest of their lives. In addition, a fully ordained person in the Zen Buddhist tradition, as practiced in Rochester, vows to dedicate his or her life to the Buddhadharma, and in receiving the ordination robes vows to use them for the welfare of all beings. Something about this level of ordination is difficult to put into words. It resembles the difference between living with someone and getting married. When one is fully ordained the commitment is greater, although the precepts we take are the same.

Because this commitment is intended to be life-long, the full ordination is approached in stages. First one receives the novice ordination, in which the same precepts are taken and one's hair is cut, but neither the robes nor the ordination name are given. A trial period follows, during which the novice must live as an ordained person but can choose not to take the final ordination or even to return to lay life. By the same token, the teacher can choose not to give the final ordination or to delay it.

Taking lay ordination simply requires the firm wish to do so, but reaching the point of taking novice ordination demands much more. At the Rochester Zen Center one must have reached a certain level of practice and kept the full practice schedule while living at the Center for a minimum of two years. One then requests one's teacher to grant the ordination. The teacher usually ignores or refuses any number of requests to test the student's seriousness and dedication. After receiving novice ordination, one continues to practice and live in the community, and after a year or two, one's progress is evaluated to determine if full ordination will be given.

I have had the honor of shaving the heads of some women before their novice ordination. We do the main shaving privately, first shaving a big Zen circle on her head. The circle is important in Zen Buddhism, the clip on our robes also being circular. It symbolizes our Buddha nature, which, like a circle, is perfect just as it is; one cannot add to or take away from it.

Then, we shave the rest of her hair, except for a tiny topknot that the teacher will cut during the ordination ceremony.

After bathing in solitude in a traditional Japanese bath scented with incense for the occasion, the novice-to-be dresses in a white underkimono. Then, in the ceremony proper, she goes before the teacher and after repenting her wrongdoings, is given the first robe. A pause occurs as we go back and help her put it on. When she returns, she prostrates in turn before the senior member of the ordained sangha, her parents, the invited lay people, and the rest of the sangha. She then goes before the teacher, who shaves off the little topknot of hair with the words, "Now the appearance is ruined." She receives the rest of her clothing—the outer robe and so on—puts them on, takes the precepts, and does more prostrations. Following this is a grand dinner for the sangha and guests to celebrate the joyful occasion.

One woman's parents came from Germany for her ordination, the first parents of a Westerner being ordained at Sogen-ji to do so. Most Western parents are somewhat aghast when their child chooses to abandon a promising career, shave her head, and wear strange clothes for the rest of her life. When I was ordained in Rochester, my two children, now adults, came, which made me very happy. My parents and siblings for various reasons did not. I do not believe my mother ever came to terms with my ordination before she died, but my father and I experienced a wonderful meeting of hearts recently. I was deeply touched that he was finally able to accept my decision and my way of life completely.

Many Westerners eventually accept the ordination of a family member. As more of us take these robes, it will become more acceptable. My children grew up in Buddhist countries and went to temples with the Buddhist nanny who worked for us. So when their mother was ordained as a Buddhist— something no other American mother does—my children were fine with it. Their support touched me deeply.

People often ask me why I became a priest. I have tried to put words to that feeling ever since it happened and have not been able to do it. The best I can say is that I was searching for something as a child. When I was nine years old, my grandmother gave me a Bible with my name engraved in gold on it. I set up an altar under the basement stairs in our house in Cleveland and searched through that Bible for meaning; but it was beyond me in those days. As I grew up, my family wanted me to become an art teacher, which I did, and then went into graphic design, architecture, and engineering, all of which I enjoyed. I raised a family, which was fulfilling; but something was still missing. Finally, I encountered Zen Buddhism and after ten years was ordained. At that time, everything fell into place. This was right for me: the square peg finally found the square hole after trying to fit in round holes all my life. I have never regretted this decision, even for a second.

I know lay people in the Rochester Zen Center and in Sogen-ji who are just as dedicated to practice. I think the difference might be that I have committed the rest of my life to it; I am not going to do anything else. I will not go back to engineering or architecture, though I may do some in the process of whatever my Dharma work is.

Becoming enlightened is a personal possibility for everybody. Everyone is there already; it is simply a matter of uncovering our misperceptions, cleaning our glasses, and seeing clearly what is already there—that we are already just as perfect as that circle, except that due to delusion and our misperceptions, we act otherwise. I would like to close with Dai E Zenji's "Vow for Awakening":

> Our only prayer is to be firm in our determination to give
> ourselves completely to the Buddha's Way, so that no doubts
> arise however long the road seems to be. To be light and

easy in the four parts of our body, to be strong and undismayed in body and in mind. To be free from illness, and drive out both depressed feelings and distractions. To be free from calamity, misfortune, harmful influences, and obstructions. Not to seek the Truth outside of ourselves, so we may instantly enter the right way. To be unattached to all thoughts, that we may reach the perfectly clear bright mind of prajna wisdom and have immediate enlightenment on the great matter of birth and death. Thereby we receive the transmission of the deep wisdom of the Buddhas to save all sentient beings who suffer in the round of birth and death. In this way we offer our gratitude for the compassion of the Buddhas and patriarchs. Our further prayer is not to be extremely ill or to suffer at the time of departure. To know its coming seven days ahead so that we may quiet the mind to abandon the body and be unattached to all things at the last moment, wherein we return to the Original Mind in the realm of no birth and no death, and merge infinitely into the whole universe to manifest as all things in their true nature and, with the great wisdom of the Buddhas, to awaken all beings to the Buddha Mind. We offer this to all Buddhas and bodhisattva-mahasattvas of the past, present, and future, in the ten quarters and to the Maha Prajnaparamita.

THE NUNS' TEACHING

FINDING OUR WAY

❖

Bhikshuni Thubten Chodron

Karen K. Shertzer

Bhikshuni Thubten Chodron graduated from UCLA, taught elementary school, and pursued graduate courses in Education. In 1975, she began practicing Buddhism with Zopa Rinpoche and later studied with Tsenzhab Serkong Rinpoche. In 1977, she received sramanerika ordination and in 1986, bhikshuni ordination. *She studied and worked as spiritual director at Istituto Lama Tzong Khapa and Dorje Pamo Monastery in Europe, and was the resident teacher at Amitabha Buddhist Centre in Singapore. She currently teaches at Dharma Friendship Foundation in Seattle. Her books include* Open Heart, Clear Mind.

U NDERSTANDING WHAT DHARMA PRACTICE IS CAN BE DIFFICULT, AND I HAVE MADE MANY MISTAKES TRYING TO FOLLOW THE PATH. Although I meant well and thought I was practicing properly at the time, only later did I come to see my misunderstandings. My hope is that by sharing these with you, you may avoid them. However, that may not be possible, because in some cases, we only learn by going through the difficulties ourselves and confronting the pain and confusion of our fixed attitudes. This certainly is true for me.

One mistake I made was assuming that because I understood the words of the Dharma, I understood their meaning. For example, I thought that my Dharma practice was developing well, because when I lived in India, I didn't get angry very much. After some time, my teacher sent me to live at a Dharma center in Italy, where I was the only American nun among a group of macho Italian monks. You can imagine the conflicts we had! But I couldn't figure out why I was having problems because I thought my patience had matured. Every evening I would study chapter six of Shantideva's text *Guide to a Bodhisattva's Way of Life*, which dealt with patience, and every day I would again get mad at the people around me. Although I knew the words of Shantideva's text well and thought I was practicing them properly, my mind continued to blame others for all the conflicts and problems.

It took me a long time to figure out what practicing patience meant, and I am still working on it. Whenever people live together there are conflicts, simply because people see things in different ways. When I lived in the nunnery in France, I handled my anger by sitting on my meditation cushion and contemplating patience. I never thought to approach the other person and say, "The way the situation appears to me is like this. How do you see it?" and to listen and discuss openly what had happened. I thought that since the cause of suffering was in my own mind, only meditation would solve the problem. Meanwhile, I was convinced that my version of the story was the one right one, and if I just did one of the mental juggling acts that Shantideva taught, the anger would go away. But all my mental juggling acts were intellectual machinations and didn't touch my anger.

Years later, I attended a workshop on communication skills and conflict resolution. It became clear that when I was angry, I could do other things besides withdrawing from the situation and meditating. Of course, we have to look at our mind and develop patience, but we can also discuss the problem with the other person. We can share how we feel in a situation without blaming the other person for our feelings. I began to understand that I had to make more effort to communicate and that I could learn a lot by opening up and discussing things with other people. This can sometimes be scary, and I still find it difficult to go to a person and say, "There's a problem here. Let's talk about it." However, I see that developing good communication skills and meditating on patience and compassion go hand in hand. If I approach the other person, deeply listen to them, and understand his or her experience, my anger automatically dissipates and compassion arises.

We may wonder: Why do we need to learn communication and conflict resolution skills? If we develop an altruistic intention (bodhicitta), won't these skills naturally arise? No, a bodhisattva does not automatically know how to do everything; he or she must still train in many skills. For example, having an altruistic intention does not mean one knows how to fly an airplane. One has to learn that skill. Similarly, although bodhicitta gives us an excellent foundation, we still need to learn skills for communicating with others, resolving conflicts, mediating disputes, and so on. The internal attitude of bodhicitta is complemented well by practical communication skills.

INDIVIDUALISM AND COMMUNITY LIFE

The Buddha established the sangha for several reasons. One is that he wanted monks and nuns to support, encourage, and help each other on the path. He set up a community so that we could learn from each other, so that we do not become isolated individuals doing whatever we fancy. For this reason, many of our precepts deal with how to live together harmoniously as a community and how to admonish each other so that we have to face our rationalizations and excuses. Thus the sangha community is a mirror helping us to purify our mind and to grow in compassion, tolerance, and understanding.

We frequently have difficulty distinguishing between our individualism and our individuality. The former is the self-centered pursuit of individual rather than collective interests. It is closely linked to self-grasping and self-centeredness, two of our principal obstructions. Adhering to our individualism makes living in community a trial for ourselves and others. Our individuality, on the other hand, is our unique combination of various qualities. In Dharma practice we learn to discriminate between qualities that are realistic and beneficial and those that are not. Then we set about increasing the former and applying the antidotes to the latter. In this way, we develop and use our individuality for the benefit of both ourselves and others.

Our Western cultural conditioning often results in confusion between individualism and individuality. Thus, we may find it difficult to follow our teachers' advice or to live together with other sangha members, because we feel our individuality and autonomy are being threatened, when really only our self-centered individualism is at stake. When we live in community, we realize we are full of opinions about everything from how fast to chant in our group ceremonies to how to realize emptiness. If we hold tightly onto our own ideas, neglecting to see that they are simply opinions and not reality, we find being with other people quite miserable because they seldom agree with us! We need to be aware that being ordained involves re-socialization and gradually relinquishing our stubborn, closed-minded individualism. Monastic training—learning to think and act like a monastic—is designed to accomplish this.

While in Taiwan to receive the bhikshuni ordination, I observed my individualism very clearly. The thirty-two day training program, culminating in the three ordinations of sramanerika, bhikshuni, and bodhisattva, is extremely strict. Everyone must do the same thing at the same time in the same way. The juniors must listen to and follow the instructions of the seniors. Each morning, before receiving teachings, all five hundred monastics had to file into the main hall and from there file into the teaching hall. In my eyes, this was a waste of time, and I saw another way to do it that would save time by filing directly into the teaching hall. With my American emphasis on efficiency, I wanted to "fix the problem." But there were some difficulties: first, I did not speak Chinese, and second, even if I had, the elders would not have been particularly interested in hearing my solution, because their method worked for them. This forced me to do something quite difficult: be quiet and do things somebody else's way. Such an insignificant situation put me face to face with my American fix-it mentality and my Western individualism. It forced me to learn to be content and to cooperate in doing things another way.

Accepting and rejoicing in the positive aspects of our own and others' individuality are important. For example, each of our Dharma sisters and brothers will have his or her own way of practicing. Not everyone will practice the way we do. Variety does not mean we have to judge one as better than the others. It simply reflects that each person has his or her own inclination and disposition. We should not compete with other practitioners. We do not need to feel inadequate because others are doing things that we are not able to. For example, some nuns are Vinaya scholars. I am interested in Vinaya but am not an expert in it. Yet I am delighted that some nuns are learned in this area because we need nuns who specialize in Vinaya and we can learn from them. Some nuns are meditators and do years of retreat. I am not ready to do a long retreat—I need to accumulate more positive potential and purify more before I can do that. But I am so glad there are nuns who do long retreat. I am happy there are nuns working in hospices and health care, nuns teaching children, and nuns organizing Buddhist events. I cannot do all those things but I rejoice that others can. Each of us will express her devotion to the Three Jewels and her gratitude to sentient beings in a different way, and the world needs all of them. If there were only meditators or scholars or social workers, the Dharma would not be round and full. We need everyone to express her practice in her individual way, and we need to say to one another, "Thank you. I'm so glad you're doing that."

CULTURAL FORMS AND THE ESSENCE OF THE DHARMA

Of the five hundred people ordained in 1986 in Taiwan, only two of us were Westerners. For the first two weeks, no one translated for us except for a few kind Chinese nuns who summarized the proceedings for us during the breaktimes. For those two weeks, the two of us went to all the sessions in a full daily program barely understanding what we were doing. For me, as a college graduate, to do something I did not understand and to be content with learning about it gradually was very difficult. Because I wanted very much to receive the bhikshuni vow, I was forced to give up my arrogant attitude and accept the situation.

Because I was present for many hours at events that I did not understand, I began to look at what subsequently has become an important issue for me: what is culture and what is Dharma? Having finally mastered many Tibetan customs, I was now in a Chinese monastery where the customs were different. Both of these traditions are Buddhist; yet superficially, in terms of dress, language, and ways of doing things, they are different. What significance does this have for me as a Westerner? What in my training as a nun is due to the culture of the countries where Buddhism has resided for centuries and what is the actual Dharma that transcends culture? What is the essence of the Buddha's teachings that we must practice, bring back to our Western countries, and teach others? What is cultural form that we need not bring to the West?

For me, this topic is of crucial importance and is a work in progress. My conclusion so far is that the Four Noble Truths, love, compassion, the altruistic intention of bodhicitta, and the wisdom realizing emptiness are the essence of the Dharma. These cannot be seen with the eyes; the understanding exists in our heart. The real Dharma is developed within our mind, and the forms are skillful tools that exist within each culture. We must be able to distinguish these so that we develop the real Dharma within ourselves and do not fool ourselves into thinking we are good practitioners simply because we are surrounded with Asian items.

For many years, I tried to act like the Tibetan nuns—shy, self-effacing, sweet. But it didn't work. Why? Because I was from a different culture and had a different upbringing than the Tibetan nuns. In school I was taught to express my thoughts, to doubt and question, to think on my own, and to be articulate. I had to confront the fact that copying a cultural form and others' external behavior was not necessarily practicing the Dharma; it was simply squeezing myself to conform to a particular personality type or culture that I had idealized as being "real Buddhism." I began to notice that my teachers had very different personalities: some were introverted, others outgoing; some were serious, others laughed a lot. Within the context of our different, constantly changing and illusive personalities, we practice the Dharma by being aware of our motivations, attitudes, and preconceptions, developing the realistic and beneficial ones, and applying the antidotes to the destructive and unrealistic ones. This work is done internally. External forms, which are involved with one culture or another, are prompts to stimulate this.

The issue of culture and essence kept following me. As resident teacher at Amitabha Buddhist Centre in Singapore, I found myself, an American, teaching Chinese to chant prayers in Tibetan, a language which none of us understood. The Tibetan chanting sounded nice and our Tibetan masters were pleased with our chanting, but we were not practicing the Dharma because we did not understand what we were saying. Although the translation process will take years and extend well beyond our lifetimes, it is essential. In time, masters will write prayers directly in our Western languages. People with musical ability will write melodies for the prayers, and we will have beautiful liturgy in our own languages.

As time went by, I began to see that, having lived in the Tibetan community for so long, I had developed a "cultural inferiority complex." When I initially left America to live in the East, I felt the West was corrupt and hoped Eastern ways would be better. But, try as I might, I could never act or think like a proper Tibetan, and began to lose my self-confidence. After many years, I realized that this loss of respect for my culture-of-origin was neither a healthy nor a productive attitude. Self-confidence is essential for a successful Dharma practice. This meant I had to see both the good and bad points of the Western culture I grew up in, as well as the good and bad points of the Tibetan culture. Comparing the two and judging one inferior and the other superior—no matter which one came out on top— was not productive. Because most of us Western monastics are operating cross-culturally, we would benefit from adopting the positive aspects and values of all the cultures we contact, while leaving behind whatever prejudices and preconceptions we may encounter.

After many years of living in Asia, I came back to the United States. It was important for me to reconnect in a positive way with the culture in which I grew up. We need to be at peace with our past, not to reject or ignore it. For me that meant acknowledging both the good and bad qualities of my background and culture and freeing my mind from either attachment or aversion to it.

Similarly, it is important to make peace with the religion we learned as a child. Having a negative attitude about our childhood religion indicates we are still bound by it, for our minds are closed and trapped in aversion. Although the religion of our childhood may not have met our spiritual needs, we did learn useful values from it. It got us going on the spiritual path, and it is important to appreciate its good points.

For me this process took an interesting turn. Having been raised Jewish, I happened to be living in Dharamsala, India, in 1990, when a Jewish delegation came to meet His Holiness the Dalai Lama, young Tibetan intellectuals, and "JuBus" (Jewish Buddhists). Meditating and talking with the Jews, I felt confident in being a Buddhist and yet happily familiar with their culture, faith, and traditions. I began to look at points in common between the two faiths and to appreciate the emphasis on ethical values, compassion, and social concern that Judaism had given me. Now, in Seattle, I participate in an ongoing Jewish-Buddhist dialogue, in which we discuss issues such as love, compassion, and suffering. In addition, Israelis have invited me to teach in their country, and in the two trips thus far, I have felt a wonderful connection with the people, helping me to explain Dharma principles and meditation techniques in a way that corresponds to their background.

Self-esteem and Self-confidence

I also misunderstood the Dharma by mistakenly using the teachings to increase my self-hatred. Meditating upon the disadvantages of self-centeredness, I would feel guilty for being so selfish, instead of seeing the selfish attitude as something separate from the nature of my mind. Eventually it became clear that whenever I meditated and felt worse about myself, I was misinterpreting the teachings and not applying them correctly. The Buddha's purpose in teaching topics such as the lower realms of rebirth and the disadvantages of self-centeredness was not to increase our despondency. Rather, he wanted us to see clearly the disadvantages of cyclic existence and its causes so that we would generate the determination to free ourselves and others from them.

Feelings of low self-esteem and inadequacy are prevalent in Westerners. In 1990, I was an observer at a conference of Western scientists and scholars with His Holiness the Dalai Lama in Dharamsala when the topic of low self-esteem was raised. Tibetans do not have words in their language for low self-esteem and guilt, so Westerners' problems with these feelings are not readily comprehensible to them. His Holiness had difficulty understanding how someone could not like himself. He looked around this room of educated, successful people and asked, "Who feels low self-esteem?" Everyone looked at each other and replied, "We all do." His Holiness was shocked and asked us the causes of this feeling. Brainstorming, we found reasons ranging from parents not holding their children enough, to the doctrine of original sin, to competition in school.

Our difficulty with self-esteem can also be linked to our emphasis on perfection and our wish to be the best, attributes that Western society teaches us to have. Caught in this conditioning, we sometimes misinterpret the Dharma: we think the perfection of ethical discipline, for example, is living up to an external standard imposed on us by others, similar to the ten commandments. However, the Dharma is not about striving for externally defined perfection to please our guru or the Buddha the way we previously tried to be good and please God. Practicing Dharma does not involve twisting ourselves into psychological knots to become our own or anyone else's ideal of the perfect monastic. Rather, the Dharma concerns looking inside ourselves and understanding all the various processes that comprise us. We come to see that our actions bear results and that if we want happiness, we need to create the causes for it by following the Dharma path, that is, by applying the meditations to diminish our disturbing attitudes and develop our good qualities.

Low self-esteem, leading to discouragement, is a hindrance on the path, for it becomes a form of laziness preventing us from making joyous effort in our practice. Thus, His Holiness has continued to explore the issue of low self-esteem and to propose Dharma antidotes to it. First, we must understand that the very nature of our mind is free from defilements. In other words, disturbing attitudes and negative emotions are like clouds that obscure the sky-like nature of mind but are not an inherent part of it. This basic purity of mind is a valid basis for having self-confidence. Not depending on external circumstances, it does not fluctuate, and thus we do not need to worry about the basis of our self-confidence disintegrating. Therefore, we can and should respect and care for ourselves. In fact, the path involves learning to care for ourselves in a proper, balanced way, not in a self-preoccupied or self-defeating way. To become a bodhisattva, we need a sense of a strong self, but this differs greatly from the self-grasping ignorance that is the root of cyclic existence. This valid sense of an efficacious conventional self enables us to be joyful and energetic in practicing the path.

In addition, we must recognize the positive factors in our lives right now. Instead of lamenting about the few things in our lives that do not correspond to our wishes, we need to focus on the positive circumstances, such as the fact that we have a human body and human intelligence. In addition, we have encountered the Dharma and qualified teachers to guide us, and we have interest in spiritual issues. If we contemplate all these fortunate circumstances and the outstanding results that can come from Dharma practice, our mind will no longer be interested in self-deprecating thoughts.

Another antidote to low self-esteem is compassion, which enables us to accept ourselves and to have a sense of humor about our foibles while simultaneously endeavoring to remedy them. While low self-esteem causes us to spiral inwards and think predominantly about ourselves, compassion—the wish for all beings, including ourselves, to be free of suffering—opens our heart to recognize the universality of the wish for happiness and freedom from suffering. Our attention then shifts from the unhealthy self-preoccupation of low self-esteem to a caring attitude that feels connected to all others on a deep level. Such an attitude naturally gives us a sense of joy and purpose in life, thus increasing our self-confidence.

LIVING THE PRECEPTS

Receiving and trying to live in accordance with the bhikshuni precepts has had considerable impact on me. In 1986, when I was ordained as a bhikshuni, there were only a handful of Western bhikshunis. For years prior to that I prayed to be able to receive these precepts because I wanted to practice and preserve the monastic lifestyle which had helped me so much.

The training program for the bhikshuni ordination in Taiwan lasted thirty-two days. It was difficult being in a foreign country, where I did not know the language or the customs. Standing hour after hour in the heat to attend training sessions and rituals that were in Chinese was not easy; but the strength of my wish to receive the ordination helped me to go through the difficulties. As we rehearsed the ordination ceremony, we gradually came to understand it, so that the actual ceremony became very powerful. At that moment, I felt the wave of blessing that comes from joining the lineage of nuns who have practiced the Dharma for over twenty-five hundred years, from the time of the Buddha until the present. This created a new sense of confidence in myself and in the practice. In addition, it increased my mindfulness, for it was the kindness of my teachers and the lay people who supported me that gave me this opportunity. My way of repaying their kindness was by trying to keep the precepts well and transform my mind.

The ordination connected me not only to all the nuns of the past, but also to all the nuns that are yet to come. I realized that I had to take responsibility for future generations of nuns. I could no longer stay in my childlike state and complain, "Why do nuns face difficult conditions? Why doesn't anyone help the nuns?" I had to grow up and take responsibility for improving not only my own situation, but also that of future generations. I came to see that practicing Dharma is not simply doing my own personal studies and practice; it is preserving something very precious so that others can have access to it.

HOW TO RELY ON A SPIRITUAL FRIEND

BHIKSHUNI JAMPA CHOKYI

*B*orn in Spain in 1945, Bhikshuni Jampa Chokyi obtained a degree in Law. She became a sramanerika in 1973 and studied with Lama Yeshe. In 1987, she received the bhikshuni vow in Hong Kong. An artist, she also translates Dharma texts and prefers to live in retreat when possible. She was co-organizer of Life as a Western Buddhist Nun.

WE KNOW WE NEED GUIDANCE ON THE PATH TO ENLIGHTENMENT, AND IT IS A SPIRITUAL FRIEND—A GURU OR A LAMA—WHO CAN PROVIDE THIS. Before exploring the various ways of understanding the guru, it is helpful to understand the Buddhist objects of refuge.

There are two types of refuge objects: the outer or causal and the inner or resultant Three Jewels. The various Buddhist traditions—Theravada, Mahayana, and Vajrayana—have slightly different ways of describing these. Regarding the outer refuge, the Theravada tradition considers the Buddha to be Shakyamuni, the historical Buddha; the Dharma to be the Three

Baskets, of which the core teaching is the Four Noble Truths; and the Sangha to be the noble ones who have realized selflessness: those at the eight levels of the path from stream-enterer to arhat. For the practitioners of this tradition, the guru or teacher is a person who explains the teachings, give precepts, and so forth. In the Mahayana tradition, the Buddha Jewel refers to all the Buddhas, whose qualities and realizations are similar to those of Shakyamuni. The Dharma is expanded to include the meaning of the Mahayana sutras, and the Sangha contains the bodhisattvas as well. In the Vajrayana or Tantra, the guru (lama) becomes even more important and is included in the objects of refuge: "I take refuge in the Gurus, the Buddhas, the Dharma, and the Sangha." Here, the guru is considered to be the embodiment of the Three Jewels, not a fourth object of refuge. The guru is the Buddha, the guru is the Dharma, and the guru is the Sangha.

From the point of view of the Sutrayana—the Theravada and general Mahayana—the lama is someone who gives teachings and guides our practice. There is a relationship between teacher and disciple, but leaving one teacher and relying on another is not a serious problem as long as the student does not have anger or contempt toward the teacher. However, when we receive Tantric initiation, the relationship between the lama and disciple is something very deep, very subtle. Once we have made such connection with a lama, breaking it is very serious.

The Tibetan Buddhist traditions emphasize that without strong guru devotion it is impossible to gain any spiritual realizations. There are many stories about the incredible hardships that great masters such as Naropa, Marpa, and Milarepa went through in order to follow their gurus' advice. Naropa's guru asked him to do some seemingly outrageous actions, such as jumping from a roof and stealing food. Marpa had to go through great pains to collect enough gold to journey to India and to make offerings to his guru, Naropa. Nowadays we may complain about having to pay for receiving teachings, but in previous times, in order to acknowledge the value of both the teacher and the teachings, disciples made lavish offerings to their gurus whenever they could. Milarepa spent six years building houses for his teacher Marpa, only to be ordered to destroy them and to start again.

A teaching in the Kagyu tradition says, "You should see everything that the guru does as perfect. If the guru kills, he is sending the consciousness of that being to a pure realm. If the guru steals, he is using material possessions to help others," and so forth. This kind of teaching may be difficult for us to understand. Another more rational approach is to check a guru carefully. If he or she tells us to do something that is in accordance with the Dharma, we should follow the advice, otherwise we should not. This accords with the Buddha's instruction: "You should not accept anything because I said so, but check it well first. Then, if you find that it is right and logical, you can accept it." However, all those highly realized beings who attained enlightenment had to follow their guru's instructions even when the guru did or told them to do outrageous things. However, as His Holiness the Dalai Lama points out, those disciples were highly realized beings who understood the subtle and hidden meanings of these instructions, while we have not yet attained their level of realization.

The Buddha also said that we should rely on the teachings, not on the teacher, and we may feel that there is a contradiction here. On the one hand, we are told that we won't achieve any realization unless we totally devote ourselves to our guru, no matter what he says, no matter what he does. On the other hand, we are told to check the teacher's advice very carefully and to consider the teachings more important than the teacher. How do we deal with this apparent contradiction? My opinion is that, regarding the guru who gives sutra teachings, we would be wiser to rely on the teachings than on the teacher; but after receiving Tantric initiations and teachings from a guru, we have to see him or her as Buddha and as more important than the meditational deities.

Some Westerners seem to have problems in their relationship with their teachers even without receiving Tantric teachings. Some of us come to Buddhism because we have many emotional problems in our life, not because we want to learn Buddhist philosophy and attain enlightenment. We just want someone to take care of us. Tibetans are more independent and stronger; they go to the Dharma because they want to learn the Dharma and not because they want to hang around a lama. Many Westerners, when they find a lama who is kind to them, totally devote themselves to him or her without checking their own minds any further. They only care about "what my lama says." In those cases, although we may call the teacher an object of refuge, he or she has become another object of our emotional problems. We give up our family and friends just to follow the lama because we need to have a safe emotional relationship with someone. Sometimes we rely on the lama because we don't want to think for ourselves. It is easier to think, "I'll just do what my guru wants." We may think this is devotion, but in fact it is just confusion. Devotion does not mean continuously following the teacher around and asking where to go, what to study, and even what to eat and what to wear. Real devotion is to practice pure Dharma in accordance with the Buddha's teachings and the lama's instructions.

We all have our inner wisdom, our inner guru. The role of the outer guru is to help us to bring forth our own Buddha mind. To some extent the guru can be considered as a parent, but only on a very high or subtle level, and certainly not on an emotional level. His job is not to take care of us like our father or our mother did.

Our teachers act as a mirror. When we seek advice, they show us exactly what is in our mind, like a mirror reflecting back what is there. They may give advice and help, but basically they are just there without projecting anything from their side. They perceive what we are projecting and show it to us. In this case, what our guru tells us to do is what we ourselves want to do, but we may not have the courage or wisdom to admit it to ourselves. At other times, the guru may tell us to do something, not because he actually wants us to do that, but because he wants us to learn how to use our own wisdom and become strong enough to make our own decisions. In this case, he is using skillful means to help us develop that inner wisdom. However, such skillful means may not be easy to understand unless we have gone through the experience ourselves.

His Holiness the Dalai Lama mentioned that when a fully qualified teacher and a fully qualified disciple, such as Tilopa, Naropa, Marpa, or Milarepa meet, enlightenment comes very easily. Instead of having unrealistic expectations of our relationship with our guru, we should ask ourselves, "Am I capable of following a teacher in the same way as those beings who attained high realizations?" To have such devotion is really wonderful, but for most of us ordinary people, it is difficult. We may have a perfect teacher, but if we are not fully qualified disciples, limitations exist. Therefore, in addition to checking the teacher's qualities carefully before entrusting ourselves to him or her, it is necessary to attentively check our minds before following the guru's advice. Otherwise, we may later regret what we did and develop a negative attitude toward the teacher and even toward the Buddha and the Dharma. This is definitely detrimental for our spiritual progress.

As we develop our awareness of who we are and what we need, we will be able to find the answers inside ourselves and will not need to rely so heavily on the advice of a lama. Also, the more we develop genuine meditative experience and get in touch with the subtle levels of our own mind, the less we need to rely emotionally on an external guru. The outer guru is definitely necessary at the beginning of our practice, but the more we meditate and learn to watch our mind, the more self-reliant we become. Through meditation we find that the guru is in our heart and everywhere.

However, that does not mean that we neglect the external guru. To reach the point where we don't need any more help from the external guru is extremely difficult, and even high lamas go to their own gurus for advice. At the moment, we are full of delusions, and we should remember that the external guru is there to show us the actual state of our present mind so that we can make efforts to transform it. We must be able to keep a balance: on one hand, we should develop our own wisdom and not rely emotionally on a guru; on the other, we should keep in mind that the connection with a guru is extremely important. By taking refuge, praying to our gurus, and visualizing them as our meditational deity, we will receive their guidance and the answers we seek. We will know what to do with our lives.

Some people may feel that relying on more than one teacher may become a source of conflict. It is helpful to remember that many highly realized beings such as Atisha, Tsong Khapa, and so forth, followed many teachers and respected all of them equally. It is not a matter of having just one guru in the same way that one has only one boyfriend at a time! In addition, meditation facilitates our understanding of the nature of all our gurus in a non-contradictory way. The essence of all our gurus is the same, although they appear as different beings and the level of their realizations may also vary. When we gain some insight into the real nature of the mind, we will discover that the true essence of our mind and the nature of our guru are the same: clear light and emptiness. We are no longer able to define a boundary between them. At that point, there is no more problem because we know that by relying on one guru we are actually relying on all of them. However, if we do not meditate and only rely on the external guru, there may seem to be a conflict between the advice of different teachers. In such a case, we should know which of our teachers we consider as the principal one and follow his or her advice.

To advance in our Dharma practice we must practice meditation. Studying, teaching, and organizing events are worthwhile activities, but they bring limited benefit. In my own case, after spending many years doing retreats, living very close to my lamas, and doing various works for them, I had the opportunity to study more. I heard the teaching on the five paths and thirty-seven factors concordant with enlightenment from Geshe Sonam Rinchen; he made it very clear that unless we develop one-pointedness of mind and bodhicitta, we do not even enter the first path. That really gave me a shock. I realized that even after all those years spent in Dharma practice, I had not even entered the actual path of Dharma. It is only through meditation based on proper study and understanding of the teachings that we can generate realizations. Thus, my wish is to meditate as much as I am able and to use whatever other activities I engage in as means to purify my delusions and accumulate merit, so that I can realize all the stages of the path and be able to help others. At the present moment, even though I may think I am helping others, that is just talking in space. Until I have genuine realizations and develop wisdom, any help I give is limited.

Let me finish with a short dedication prayer written by His Holiness the Fifth Dalai Lama:

The outer lama is the various Bodies of Transformation.
The inner lama is the All Pure Heruka (the Body of Enjoyment).
The secret lama is our basic, most subtle mind.
Please bless me to meet these three lamas in this very lifetime.

BRINGING A PSYCHOLOGICAL PERSPECTIVE TO THE DHARMA

Bhikshuni Wendy Finster

*B*orn in Australia, Bhikshuni Wendy Finster has an M.A. in Applied Psychology, and is a clinical psychologist with both clinical and academic research interests. A student of Lama Yeshe and Zopa Rinpoche, she received sramanerika vows in 1976 and bhikshuni vows in the late 1980s in Taiwan. She lived and taught in Buddhist centers in Australia and Italy. She currently lives in Australia where she teaches the Dharma, is a psychotherapist, and conducts research on treatment modalities for people with chronic health problems.

THE POINTS OF CONTACT BETWEEN BUDDHADHARMA AND WESTERN PSYCHOLOGY ARE MANY. Yet, we must be able to distinguish between the two and know how and when to use each one. I will not pretend to understand these topics with complete clarity, but will share my personal opinions and experiences, based on my training and practice as a clinical psychologist in community mental health, as well as my training and practice for twenty-two years in the Dharma. Others will have different opinions, and further discussion of these points will enrich us all.

All of us ordinary beings are, I believe, mentally unbalanced until we attain enlightenment. We are all deluded; we all have hallucinations of our own creation and believe in them, thereby creating our own little sphere of mental disturbance. From this perspective, only enlightened persons are totally mentally healthy, although bodhisattvas and arhats are well on their way. In essence, we are all a bit crazy; it is just a matter of degree.

A number of Dharma students, however, experience severe mental disturbance and unbalance at some time or another during their practice. In these instances, we must differentiate the two levels of reality: ultimate and relative. Ultimate reality and the ultimate wisdom that understands it concern the deeper mode of existence of phenomena, one that is not perceivable by our senses or our gross levels of mind. Relative reality concerns the objects and people we deal with on a daily basis. It is possible to become mentally disturbed only on a relative plane with the relative mind. It is impossible for the ultimate level of mind to become crazy. When people have some kind of difficulty, then, it is in relation to their ability to handle relative reality and to know the difference between an experience of ultimate reality and the relative plane in which they live their daily life. They are unable to differentiate between mental creations and beliefs, and the conventionally accepted external phenomenal world.

Many factors can trigger such disturbances. In my observation, some people have a certain hypersensitivity derived from past emotional or cognitive experiences, that predisposes them to mental imbalance. The use of drugs, recitation of particular mantras or too many mantras too quickly, or powerful meditation on the chakras and energies can tip the balance for such people. I also wonder if, for some people with certain personalities and energy, staying in silence for long periods and meditating without any discussion with a teacher is useful. Such forceful, sudden change from their usual way of living seems to cause tension that can trigger mental imbalance.

For example, once I was called to a meditation center where a twenty-one-year old Canadian man had become mentally disturbed. A number of Western students there were meditating under the guidance of a Burmese master. They lived in total silence except for five or ten minutes each day when they could speak about what was going on within them. I wonder if for people with a particular kind of energy, such long periods of silence accompanied by intense meditation may in fact trigger an energy explosion within them. Other students at the center had noticed that he had become withdrawn over the preceding days, but nobody even knew his name; nobody ever talked with anyone else. They felt sorry that they did not know his name and that something had been troubling him before the time he lost touch with what was going on.

In general, a person who later has mental difficulties during his or her meditation practice becomes unhappy and mentally agitated prior to the time he actually becomes dysfunctional. Then he develops fear and paranoia that can alternate with a feeling of superiority. He becomes confused and is unable to make sense of everyday things or to interact successfully with the everyday world. I have noticed that when other people in the environment treat this person in a supersensitive way, as if he were crazy, he learns that and becomes more uncontrolled. He begins to believe that he is in fact mentally disturbed and separates himself from others because of that feeling. How can we help a person in this situation?

If the person is obviously a danger to himself or others, without hesitation we should immediately take him for professional assessment and treatment. It is useful to act normally around the person, to treat him as though he is normal and things are as usual. We should talk about the way things are usually done, reminding and emphasizing how to behave on the practical plane. It is also useful for the person to be physically active, to do physical jobs such as gardening, taking care of animals, cleaning, walking in nature, or any job that requires a coordination of physical energy to produce a result. This helps the person to re-balance his sense of being in the world and to re-solidify his sense of self. We need to help him get a stronger sense of the ego. Sometimes we can say, "You are like this and that. You can do this and that very well," and thereby remind him of his skills or personality characteristics.

It is tricky, but it is also useful to try to communicate with that part of his mind that can perceive the whole scenario as a drama being created and then played out with himself as the main protagonist. One aspect of the mind sees this whole drama, and if we can help him to find and communicate with that part of the mind, it has a settling effect on him. We can also place the person in situations with which he is familiar. For example, if he happens to be away from his usual environment, we can take him to a familiar environment—his home, the community shopping center—so he is near familiar things that will bring him back to his usual sense of self.

GETTING STUCK

Although we may not suffer from severe mental problems, at times all of us feel stuck in our practice. This can happen in a variety of ways. One is by having high expectations of quick achievement and thus pushing ourselves to practice long hours, which often results in frustration, stress, or illness. If we are in touch with our body and its energy, we can know when we are pushing too hard before it becomes an obstacle. Even if we think our level of intensity is good because we seem to be more concentrated, it can cause a reverberation in our body that can make us overly emotional or even physically ill. We must let go of our unrealistic expectations and have the determination to practice over a long time. The balance of mind and body is delicate and precious, and we should take care to nourish it.

Some students practice for years but do not seem to make much progress with some heavy personal characteristics such as resentment or anger. The Dharma has tools to deal with these, but it appears they do not use them. What is missing? I believe that most of the change we make due to Dharma practice occurs by having a strong student-teacher relationship. Thus, I encourage people who are not making headway with deeply rooted personally traits to work with a qualified teacher and develop enough devotion so that they can accept the teacher's criticism and pressure to deal with that trait. If they do not have such a relationship with a teacher, I describe its benefits and suggest they try to find a good teacher with whom to work. If they do not want to do that, I encourage them to do work that would force them to face and correct that quality in themselves.

Sometimes people have a close personal relationship with a teacher and work on a daily basis with the teacher, yet do not seem to change. If a lay student, due to living in a Dharma center for many years, has lost perspective on the problems faced by others in society, I generally advise her to leave the center and live elsewhere for a while in order to experience reality in the bigger world. I encourage monastics to do purification practice and to balance their study, work, and meditation. Often we Westerners become too focused on one aspect, and this lack of balance makes us feel that we are not making progress. If we do not do retreat or have some inner experience of the Dharma, we do not feel that we are worthy sangha. Taking the time to do retreat enables us to consolidate our practice, and as a result, to experience the change within ourselves. This can carry us through the times of work and service for others.

Sometimes we are so black and white, so determined to study a particular text or do a certain practice, that push ourselves, thus becoming anxious and stressed. We often do not notice the damaging effect of this self-applied pressure until it is too late to undo easily. Thus, before beginning a retreat or a period of intense study, people need to be aware that if they start feeling too tense, they should give themselves permission to disengage from that activity and relax their mind. Later, with a happy, relaxed mind, they can return to complete the activity.

Some Western centers now have confidential registration forms for participants in retreats or intensive courses in which they ask if one takes any medication or has ever been hospitalized for mental problems. Other questions could be added to help the teacher be aware of people with potential difficulties. The teacher or an assistant could also have a personal interview with participants prior to an intensive retreat in order to discuss some of these points.

ACTING AS A COUNSELOR IN DHARMA COMMUNITIES

When people in Dharma centers or monastic communities approach us for counseling, we must first determine whether the person wants advice regarding her Dharma practice and clarification of the Buddha's teachings, or whether she wants counseling for a psychological problem. Differentiating these two is extremely important, and if the person's issue is a psychological one, we should refer her to someone capable of giving the professional help she needs.

Because I am a psychologist as well as a nun, I have often been approached by Dharma students for help with personal psychological difficulties that they want to discuss with someone who understands the Dharma. However, as someone qualified in both Dharma and psychology,

I believe it is far better not to mix roles with one person. As a monastic and a Dharma practitioner, my specialty and source of benefit is in terms of the Dharma. Therefore, I decline to enter into a therapy relationship with a Dharma student and refer them to a well-qualified therapist for help with their psychological problems.

If someone approaches us for help and we determine that it regards her Dharma practice and her way of handling the difficulty according to the Dharma, we are qualified as Dharma practitioners to give her Dharma advice. Before doing so, however, we have to create a situation conducive for giving such help. First, we must be calm and balanced, meaning that none of the three poisonous attitudes—confusion, anger, or clinging attachment—dominate or disturb our mind at that moment. We must give ourselves space to calm down, empty ourselves of our own preconceptions, and prepare for such an interview so that we can listen deeply and respond clearly. We can prevent pride from arising by recognizing that similar problems could occur in our lives while we remain in cyclic existence. Although we are temporarily in a position to offer advice to someone with difficulties, in fact we have the seeds of those same problems within us, and given certain circumstances and conditions, they could arise in our lives.

We must also ensure that the other person discovers her own answer, instead of giving her our answer. When we speak of refuge, there is outer refuge—the Buddhas, Dharma, and Sangha external to us. There is also inner refuge, our wisdom and compassion, the ultimate refuge being our own inner Dharma wisdom. Because we must enable this to grow in both ourselves and the other, our role is to help the person discover her own solution within herself. When she is able to do this, her self-confidence in growing her own Dharma wisdom and progressing along the path will increase. We must communicate optimism for change, letting her know that the potential for enlightenment is intact regardless of how disturbed her mind may be due to her habitual ways of thinking or acting.

As a Dharma counselor, we must remember that we are simply a cooperative condition for helping the other person grow; we are not a cause. We are not ultimately responsible for his growth, nor can we make him change. Understanding this and understanding karma prevents us from being over-involved and makes clear where responsibility lies.

When a person living in a community becomes mentally disturbed, we must set boundaries for acceptable behavior and ask people to leave if they are unable to comply. We need to do this with sensitivity and compassion by describing why we have community rules and why it is important that everyone follows them. If we must ask the person to leave the community, we explain, "Unfortunately, because you are experiencing some difficulties in this area, problems arise. If you live somewhere else and get help for that behavior so that you are able to deal with it, we are happy to welcome you back into the community again."

In a community of one hundred or two hundred people, one disturbed person would probably not make too many ripples. But in our small and newly begun Western communities, one mentally disturbed person in a group of five or six will destroy the harmony of the group. Our understanding of compassion is incorrect if we think that we should not point out to a person what is expected of him, where his behavior has fallen short, and his need to get help. Not dealing straightforwardly and firmly creates a type of co-dependency in which we actually encourage a person not to change.

THE INTERFACE OF BUDDHISM AND WESTERN PSYCHOLOGY

The relationship between Buddhism and Western psychological theories and techniques is an important topic concerning the spread of Buddhism in the West. Over the last ten years, many people have begun offering mixed or comparative courses that include some Dharma and some Western psychology. I doubt that it is possible to do this well unless one has equal expertise in both areas. Otherwise the points of comparison will not be at a deep level and will not be valid.

The factors making accurate comparison difficult are many. First, the Buddhadharma is a vast and profound system of knowledge. In addition, many types of Western psychology and philosophy exist, each with its own areas and specialties. One needs to be extremely careful before setting oneself up as one who can do a valid comparison. I have noticed that people who have not done serious study in Western psychology, and thus are not qualified to give comparative or mixed courses, are often asked to do so. These people may have read a few books and taken some experiential courses that awakened exciting personal insights, and in the process think they can create and teach a course in this. I find this quite surprising: I am a clinical psychologist and a Buddhist nun, yet I do not feel I can do justice to such a comparison or integration. Similarly, some psychologists, having gone to a few Buddhist retreats and read some books, believe they are qualified to teach meditation and Dharma to other psychologists or their clients. There are, however, generic forms of meditation that can be useful for introducing those in therapy to their inner world.

I personally find it interesting to look at the parallels between Buddhism on the one hand and Western psychology and philosophy on the other. However, I do not believe a Dharma center is the appropriate place for that exploration to take place. People can go to many other places in the West to attend psychology courses or support groups, or to hear lectures on mixed disciplines. When people go to a Dharma center, they should receive the pure Buddhadharma, which is a complete system guiding a person all the way to enlightenment. When it is taught purely, the essence and principles of Buddha's teachings can be applied by the individual according to his or her particular context and needs. However, the Dharma teaching itself should not be changed according to the flavor of the month. We are extremely fortunate that the Buddhadharma has been maintained in its pure form and passed down through lineages in many countries for thousands of years. It would be a great pity if, through our generation's carelessness, the Buddhadharma became polluted in the West by adding ideas from Western philosophy and psychology that appear to fit in.

However, Westerners who come to Buddhism do have different issues than the Asians who have held and passed the teachings on all these years. Due to our own issues, we Westerners may not be able to easily apply some of the Buddha's teachings. To make the Dharma applicable in the West, then, we have to look at the society within which we grew up, how we were conditioned, and the ideas and values held as true in the West. For example, we were raised to be individualistic and to be enthusiastic consumers. Because of our cultural conditioning, we often create unrealistic expectations of both ourselves and others, and these generate frustration and anger when things do not turn out the way we wanted. I think these expectations are related to our yearning for perfection; and this yearning is a pitfall because when we start looking for perfection, we cannot find it. This causes us to judge ourselves harshly and feel guilty, and as a result, our self-esteem plummets. This surprises our Asian teachers; they do not realize the level of self-criticism and self-hatred that can arise in individuals raised in our culture. Westerners tend to feel fear, anxiety, and insecurity, which leads to competition, and this, in turn, produces a type of paranoia that underlies all our experience.

The conditioning we receive in the first seven years of our lives has great impact on us, affecting us on gross and subtle levels. The family into which we were born, the experiences we had at school, the values that were emphasized, and the expectations of the nation and culture all affect our outlook as adults. In the same way, children who grow up in Asia imbibe from the time they are small the belief that this is one of many lives and that offering to the sangha creates great merit. Although such concepts are alien to Westerners, they feel comfortable and are easily accepted by those who grew up in a culture with that prevailing norm. Exploring more deeply the effects of our conditioning could help us progress along the Dharma path. This should be done at a place that specializes in conventional mental health and personal development programs. If the personnel at the Dharma center feel it appropriate to offer such mental health courses themselves, the most appropriate way would be to offer the courses in other locations and perhaps set up a subsidiary branch of the Dharma center to run the courses in those places. I strongly feel that when people go to a Buddhist center, they should know what they will receive, and that should be the Buddhadharma, not somebody's compilation of bits and pieces of this and that mixed in with the Dharma.

MISUNDERSTANDING THE BUDDHA'S TEACHINGS

In some cases, the Buddha's teachings have been misused or misunderstood in the West. One example is spiritual materialism, a term coined by Trungpa Rinpoche. In gross form, this occurs, for instance, when Dharma students take on Tibetan cultural trappings. They wear Tibetan clothes, adopt Tibetan mannerisms, and so on. It can become quite a trip. We should be careful to distinguish between the Buddhadharma and the cultural context within which it has developed, and then be sure that we grasp the essence of the Dharma without getting caught up in paraphernalia appropriate in its Asian cultural context. We must make an effort, through our own individual practice, to separate the grain from the chaff. Within our own cultural context, the wisdom the Buddha taught can be included in the disciplines of philosophy, psychology, theology, and contemplative studies.

In a subtler form, spiritual materialism occurs when we use the Dharma to reinforce our desires, pride, or political views. For example, when we learn something and are able to teach others, we may become smug, self-satisfied, and arrogant as a result. Using the Dharma in this way is like taking poison.

A second way in which we Westerners tend to misinterpret the Dharma teachings is by believing that all feelings—or at least the troublesome ones—should be repressed or pushed away. I think this is done out of a basic dislike for oneself and self-hatred, arising due to the strong influence of Cartesian dualist thought in the West. Our language and the words we use strongly affect our ideas, philosophy, way of thinking, and what we feel is possible. We have a cultural heritage of a very powerful dualism between good and bad, with no gray area in-between. Our perfectionism comes from wanting things to be perfect in an absolute way. Asian cultures, on the other hand, do not put such stress on the extremes of good and bad, right and wrong, and see things as a gradation. In our culture, we do not have this perspective and thus can easily become inflexible.

An example of this inflexibility is a Dharma student intensely reciting mantras, while walking with prayer beads in hand in a Dharma center. Someone stops to ask her for assistance, but she cannot bring herself to break that intense concentration to help the person in front of her. Another example is someone who has studied the Dharma for years, learned all the outlines of the philosophical treatises, and passed examinations on these topics. However, his daily life actions are out of control. At a number of centers the comment has been made that non-Dharma people are often much kinder than people studying at the center. This should make us reflect: Are we truly practicing the Dharma? Or are we misusing it to fulfill our cravings or repress our problems, and in the process poisoning not only our practice but also the purity of the Dharma in the world?

An excellent yardstick for assessing our Dharma practice is to check if we are becoming happier. If we find that we are not happier in our daily life, then we are not practicing the Dharma correctly. We must be either misinterpreting or misapplying what the Buddha taught. No matter what wonderful high realizations we think we may have attained, unless we are able to translate them into kitchen sink reality and talk about them in very basic terms, we are off with the birds. One of my teachers told me, "If you do retreat and think you have had fantastic experiences and attained great realization yet you are not able to bring those experiences into your reality on earth on a day-to-day basis, you don't have any realizations. You're just on another ego trip."

It sometimes happens that a teacher, director, or other person in a position of responsibility in a Dharma center behaves erratically. When this happens, it is important to maintain our discriminative wisdom and to accurately discern right and wrong behaviors, whether they are in ourselves or in someone in a position of responsibility. In the latter case, if we discover that something inappropriate has been said or done, we need to make it known in a skillful way. We need to dissociate ourselves from that behavior, and if necessary, we may have to leave the situation. It is important to contemplate the four reliances:

1. Rely on the doctrine and not on the person teaching it
2. Rely on the meaning and not on the words
3. Rely on sutras of definitive meaning and not on those of interpretable meaning

4. Rely on the exalted wisdom directly perceiving reality and not on ordinary consciousness

Our present opportunity to learn the Buddhadharma and our freedom to practice it are unbelievably precious. Confidence in the validity of the teachings helps us to practice enthusiastically. The obvious method to determine this validity is to put the teachings into practice in our daily lives in a correct and gradual manner. If we observe results occurring with our physical, verbal, and mental actions moving in a more positive direction, we know the teachings work. Even though it is unwise to expect instant happiness and wise to be prepared to practice over many lifetimes, we should still be able to notice clear changes in our mental attitudes and our actions from year to year. Slowly our kind thoughts and compassionate actions will increase, benefiting ourselves and all those around us. We will make the heart of the Buddha's teaching come alive by following his essential instructions:

> Do not commit any unwholesome action.
> Enjoy doing perfectly constructive actions.
> Subdue your own mind completely—
> This is the teaching of the Buddha.

LIVING THE DHARMA

Khandro Rinpoche

*B*orn in 1967 in the Tibetan refugee
family of Mindroling Rinpoche, Khandro
Rinpoche received both a traditional
Tibetan education and a modern Western
one. At a young age she was recognized
as the incarnation of the Great Khandro
of Tsurphu, who was an emanation of
Yeshe Tsogyal and the consort of the
Fifteenth Karmapa. Her main spiritual teachers are Mindroling Trichen
Rinpoche, the Sixteenth Karmapa, and Dilgo Khyentse Rinpoche. Khandro
Rinpoche is a lineage holder in the Nyingma school of Tibetan Buddhism. She
heads her father's monastery, Karma Chokhor Dechen Nunnery, and Samten
Tse Retreat Center in Mussoorie. She also teaches widely in the West.

WE ALL ARE AWARE OF THE PROBLEMS WE FACE TODAY, AND
WE ARE ALSO AWARE OF THE POTENTIALS AND THE QUALITIES
PRESENT IN THE FEMALE SANGHA. When there is a talk about
women and Buddhism, I have noticed that people often regard the topic as
something new and different. They believe that women in Buddhism has
become an important topic because we live in modern times and so many

women are practicing the Dharma now. However, this is not the case. The female sangha has been here for centuries. We are not bringing something new into a twenty-five hundred-year-old tradition. The roots are there, and we are simply re-energizing them.

When women join the sangha, sometimes one part of their minds thinks, "Maybe I won't be treated equally because I am a woman." With that attitude, when we do a simple thing, such as enter a shrine room, we immediately look for either the front seat or the back seat. Those who are more proud think, "I'm a woman," and rush for the front row. Those who are less self-confident immediately head for the last row. We need to examine this kind of thinking and behavior. The foundation and essence of the Dharma goes beyond this discrimination.

Sometimes you suffer from doubt and dissatisfied mind in your Dharma practice. When you do a retreat, you wonder if bodhicitta would grow more easily from actually working with people who are suffering. You think, "What is the benefit of selfishly sitting in this room, working toward my own enlightenment?" Meanwhile, when you do work to help people, you think, "I have no time to practice. Perhaps I should be in a retreat where I can realize the Dharma." All of these doubts arise because of ego.

Dissatisfied mind arises toward the precepts as well. When you do not have precepts, you think, "The monastics have dedicated their lives to Dharma and have so much time to practice. I want to be a monastic too." Then after you become a monastic, you are also busy and begin to think that being a monastic is not the real way to practice. You start to doubt, "Perhaps it would be more realistic to stay within the world. The monastic life may be too traditional and alien for me." Such obstacles are simply manifestations of a dissatisfied mind.

Whether you are a monastic or a lay practitioner, rejoice in your practice.

Do not be rigid or worry unnecessarily about doing things wrong. Whatever you do—talking, sleeping, practicing—allow spontaneity to arise. From spontaneity comes courage. This courage enables you to make an effort to learn each day, to remain within the arising moment, and then the confidence of being a practitioner will emerge within you. That brings more happiness, which will enable you to live according to your precepts. Do not think that precepts tie you down. Rather, they enable you to be more flexible, open up, and look beyond yourself. They give you the space to practice the path of renunciation and bodhicitta. It must be understood that by taking the precepts we are able to loosen our rigid individualism in many ways and thus be more available to others.

Previously, many women lacked the confidence that they could achieve enlightenment, but I think that is not much of a problem now. Many women practitioners, lay women as well as nuns, have done incredible work. Different projects are underway and our external circumstances are improving. Nevertheless, some people ask, "How can we practice with the shortage of female role models to teach us?" I wonder: Does the teacher you dream of have to be a woman? If so, will you want to spend as much time as possible with her? Our wants and wishes never end.

I agree there is a great need for women teachers, and many young nuns are exceptional in their education today. We should definitely request them to teach. Many nuns simply need the confidence to teach and thus to help one another. To learn, you do not necessarily need a teacher who has studied thousands of texts. Someone who knows just one text well can share it. We need people who will pass onto others what they know now.

But your ego blocks you from learning and benefiting from each other. Those who could teach often doubt themselves thinking, "Who is going to listen?" And those who need to learn often look for the "highest" teacher, not the teacher with knowledge. Looking for the "perfect" teacher is sometimes a hindrance. You think, "Why should I listen to this person? I have been a nun longer than she has. I have done a three-year retreat, but she hasn't." Watch out for this type of attitude. Of course, a person who has all the qualities and can expound all the teachings properly is very important. But also realize that you are in a situation where any knowledge is appreciated. Until you meet this "perfect" teacher, try to learn wherever and whenever you can. If it is knowledge you are looking for, you will find it. People will be available to teach you, but you may lack the humility needed to be a perfect recipient.

I believe Buddhism will be Westernized. Some changes definitely need to come about, but they need to be well thought out. It is not appropriate to change something simply because we have difficulty with it. Our ego finds difficulty with almost everything! We must examine what will enable people to be more flexible, to communicate better, and to extend themselves to others, and then make changes for these reasons. Deciding what and how to change is a delicate matter and can be very tricky. We must work carefully on this and be sure to preserve the authenticity of the Dharma and keep true compassion at heart.

THE NEED FOR COMMUNITY

We in the Tibetan Buddhist tradition often become absorbed in "my vows," "my community," "my sect," "my practice," and this keeps us from putting our practice into action. As practitioners, we should not become isolated from one another. Remember that we are not practicing and are not ordained for our own convenience; we are following the path toward enlightenment and working for the benefit of all sentient beings. Being a sangha member is a hard, yet valuable responsibility. For us to make progress and our aspirations to bear fruit, we must work together and appreciate one another honestly. Therefore, we need to know one another, live together, and experience community life.

We need places where Western nuns can live and practice, just as in the East. If we sincerely want the female sangha to flourish and develop, some amount of hard work is necessary. We cannot simply let it be and say it is difficult. If problems exist, we are, more or less, responsible for them. On the other hand, good results come from working together and being unified. In Western society, you become independent at a very young age. You have privacy and can do whatever you like. Community life in the sangha immediately confronts you with living with different people who have varying opinions and views. Of course problems will arise. Instead of complaining or avoiding your responsibility when this happens, you need to bring your practice to the situation.

Constructing a place for the sangha is not too difficult, but developing trust is. When someone disciplines you, you should be able to accept it. If you want to move out the moment that you do not like something, your life as a nun will be difficult. If you think about giving back your vows every time your teacher or someone in the monastery says something you do not want to hear, how will you progress? The motivation begins with you. You must begin with a solid, sincere motivation and want to follow a path of renunciation. When you have that motivation, problems will not seem so big, and you will meet teachers and receive teachings without much difficulty.

Simply waking up as a community, walking into the shrine room as a community, practicing as a community, eating as a community is wonderful. This must be learned and practiced. The experience of living together is very different from understanding a nun's life by reading books. A teacher can say, "Vinaya says to do this and not that," and people will take notes and review the teaching. But this is not the same as living the teachings together with other people. When we actually live it ourselves, a more natural way of learning occurs.

As a sangha, we need to work together. It is important for us to help each other and to help those in positions of responsibility in whatever way we can. We also need to respect those who teach us. When a nun is well trained, she can teach other nuns. The nuns who study with her will respect her, saying, "She is my teacher." She is not necessarily their root teacher, but she has good qualities and has given them knowledge, and that is reason enough to respect her.

See that in your lifetime, you give whatever you know to at least ten people. Receiving complete teachings is difficult, so when you are fortunate enough to receive teachings, make sure to make it easier for others to get them. Help to improve the circumstances and to share what you learn so that others do not have to struggle as much as you did. When many instructions and teachings are given, we will have educated nuns who are well versed, and they will benefit many people.

THE IMPORTANCE OF MOTIVATION

Whether one is a nun, a Westerner, a Tibetan, a lay person, a meditator, or whatever, practice comes back to one thing: checking oneself. Time and time again, we need to observe very carefully what we are doing. If we find ourselves simply seeing our Dharma practice as an extracurricular activity, similar to a hobby, then we are off track.

Almost all human beings begin with good motivation. They do not begin to practice Dharma with a lack of faith or a lack of compassion. As people continue to practice, some meet favorable conditions and increase their good qualities. They gain genuine experiences through their meditation and grasp the real meaning of Dharma practice. But some who begin with inspiration, faith, and strong motivation, find after many years that they have not changed much. They have the same thoughts, difficulties, and problems as before. They appreciate and agree with the Dharma, but when it comes to practicing it and changing themselves, they find difficulties. Their own ego, anger, laziness, and other negative emotions become so important and necessary for them. Their minds make difficult circumstances seem very real, and then they say they can't practice.

If this happens to us, we have to examine: How much do we really want enlightenment? How much do we want to go beyond our negative emotions and wrong views? Looking carefully into ourselves, we may see that we want enlightenment, but we also want many other things. We want to enjoy pleasure, we want others to think that we are enlightened, we want them to recognize how kind and helpful we are. From morning to night we encounter samsara, with all its difficulties, at very close range. Yet how many of us actually want to go beyond this and leave samsara?

Genuine great compassion motivates us to attain enlightenment and benefit sentient beings. Nevertheless, we tend to use compassion and bodhicitta as excuses to indulge in what we like. Sometimes we do what ego wants, saying, "I'm doing it for the sake of others." Other times we use the excuse that we have to do our Dharma practices in order to shirk our responsibilities. But Dharma practice is not about running away from responsibilities. Instead, we need to turn away from habitual negative patterns of thought and behavior, and to discover these patterns we need to look within ourselves. Until that is done, simply speaking about the Dharma, teaching, or memorizing texts does not bring much real benefit.

You talk about compassion and benefiting sentient beings, but it must begin this moment, with the person sitting next to you, with your community. If you cannot endure a person in the room, what kind of practitioner does that make you? You should listen to teachings and put them into practice so that you change.

Faith is an essential element on the path of renunciation, on the path to enlightenment. Our faith is still comparatively superficial and therefore shakable. Small situations make us doubt the Dharma and the path, causing our determination to decline. If our motivation and faith are shakable, how can we talk about leaving behind all the karma and negative emotions that have been following us for lifetimes? Through study and practice we will begin to develop real knowledge and understanding. We will see how true the Dharma is, and then our faith will be unshakable.

In the West, people often want teachings that are enjoyable to listen to, ones which say what they want to hear. They want the teacher to be entertaining and tell amusing stories that make them laugh. Or Westerners want the highest teachings: Atiyoga, Dzogchen, Mahamudra, and Tantric initiations. People flood to these teachings. Of course, they are important, but if you do not have a strong foundation, you will not understand them, and the benefit that they are supposed to bring will not be achieved. On the other hand, when the foundation practices—refuge, karma, bodhicitta, and so forth—are taught, people often think, "I've heard that before so many times. Why don't these teachers say something new and interesting?" Such an attitude is a hindrance to your practice. You have to focus on changing your daily attitudes and behavior. If you cannot do basic practices, such as abandoning the ten negative actions, and practice the ten virtuous ones, talking about Mahamudra will bring little benefit.

Three activities are necessary. Any particular time of your life can contain all three but in terms of emphasis: first, listen to, study, and learn the teachings; second, think and reflect upon them; and third, meditate and put them into practice. Then, with a motivation to benefit others, share the teachings to the best of your capability with those who are interested and who can benefit from them.

APPENDICES

The participants of *Life as a Western Buddhist Nun* meet with His Holiness the Dalai Lama Dharamsala, India 1996

THE SITUATION OF WESTERN MONASTICS

Bhikshuni Tenzin Palmo

Born in England in 1943, Bhikshuni Tenzin Palmo joined the Buddhist Society in 1961 and went to India in 1964. There she met her principal teacher, Venerable Khamtrul Rinpoche, a Drukpa Kagyu lama, in whose community she studied and worked for six years. In 1967 she received sramanerika ordination from Gyalwa Karmapa and in 1973 bhikshuni ordination in Hong Kong. In 1970, she began a twelve-year retreat in a cave in the mountains of Lahaul, India. In 1988 she moved to Italy where she also did retreat. Now she teaches internationally and is establishing Dongyu Gatsel Nunnery in Tashi Jong, India. This paper about the situation of Western monastics ordained in the Tibetan Buddhist tradition was presented at the first Conference for Western Buddhist Teachers with His Holiness the Dalai Lama in Dharamsala, India, March 1993. It was one of the stimuli for Life as a Western Buddhist Nun.

ONASTICISM IS WONDERFUL FOR SOME PEOPLE, BUT IT IS NOT FOR EVERYBODY, NOR SHOULD IT BE. It exists for that small group of individuals who are drawn toward the ideal of a life totally dedicated to the Dharma through the renunciation of worldly concerns and through ethical purity. As we all know, modern society is based principally on greed and promotes the view that happiness depends mainly on acquisition and the satisfaction of desire. Sex and violence rage everywhere nowadays. In contrast, the sangha is a group of monastics whose lives are based on renunciation, purity, restraint, and discipline, all of which are aimed at reducing our wants and desires. What these people do goes completely against the current of the world.

Dharma centers are not immune to the idea that "more is better." Traditionally in the East, the sangha had the role of preserving and transmitting the Dharma. Because the people of those societies supported the Dharma, they respected the sangha; they loved the sangha and were very proud of their monastics. However, in the West, the situation is different partly because in modern times many of the scholars and meditation teachers who transmit the Dharma in the West are laity. This does not mean that the sangha is useless for the modern world. Because the sangha preserves a way of life based on Dharma principles, monastics are a living example that restraint and simplicity bring happiness and peace. They remind us that one can live with few possessions and without sex, family, or security and yet be happy and content. Monastics should have the time to devote to study and practice without having the material problems of earning a living or the emotional problems of entanglement in personal relationships based on attachment. The sangha has freedom—both physical and emotional— which is often not available to those who live a lay life.

Unfortunately, due to modern attitudes that stem from our Protestant and materialistic backgrounds, many Western Buddhists strongly feel that having close relationships, family, and career is a superior way of practicing the Dharma. Having these things, which are mostly objects of our attachment, is still projected by many Western Buddhists as being desirable, as well as providing a good opportunity to practice the Dharma by integrating it into daily life. Therefore, in the West, sangha members are seen as escapists, neurotics, and parasites, as people unable to face up to the challenge of intimate relationships. Renunciation is misunderstood and disparaged. In fact, some people consider it to be slightly perverse—because you cannot make it in the world, you renounce it, basically because it has renounced you.

A true monastic lives without security, dependent upon the unsolicited generosity of others. This is not being a parasite—this is going forth in faith. Jesus said, "Give ye no thought unto the morrow what ye shall eat and what ye shall wear." In a way, that is what being a member of the sangha is all about: we are not overly concerned with our physical existence and have confidence that the Dharma will provide enough for our simple needs. We have faith that if we practice sincerely, we will not starve; we will be supported not just materially, but in every way.

However, in Dharma circles in the West, the sangha lives in a kind of limbo. We are neither supported by the laity, nor by the lamas themselves. Even when monastics work for centers and are thereby supported, they are still in many ways second-class citizens. They are not given good accommodations and are treated as inferior to paying guests, who have a lot of money and can support the centers. There is very little respect or appreciation for sangha members having devoted their entire lives to the Dharma. Centers are mainly geared toward lay people and monastics are shunted to one side and considered unimportant. Or, they are overworked and expected to run centers before they have had sufficient training or experience. People expect them to be capable even if they have had little training, while they are imperfect human beings like the others.

Western sangha members also need understanding and appreciation, but they very seldom receive it. Because they often do not live in monastic communities but in Dharma centers or by themselves, they cannot do things that the lay people can do. Yet they do not have the conditions to live a monastic life either. They lose out on the pleasures of a family life, and at the same time, they have few of the joys of a true monastic life.

Some of them feel lonely; also they feel they are unable to integrate the ideals of non-attachment with seeing others as lovable. They are unsure of what friendship means in a Dharma context and feel that developing affection means becoming too involved, which is not suitable for a monastic. Because they do not have the examples of older practitioners or live in a monastic community, they do not understand how to balance the introspection necessary for Dharma practice with friendship and affection for others, which are also important for practice. Thus their practice may become sterile, and they may feel alienated from the people around them. Some feel that wearing robes alienates them from other people, that people act artificially toward them, cast them in a role, and do not see them as human beings who have problems and need moral support and friendship. Some feel conspicuous wearing robes in the street in the West because people stare and some even say, "Hare Krishna!" Because others react toward them differently, they feel they cannot help people effectively.

Western monastics receive very little support from the lamas. Your Holiness, this is true. Unlike in traditional Asian societies where the lay people naturally esteem and support the sangha, in the West, with our tradition of democracy and equality, this is not so. Western lay people are not encouraged to respect the sangha, at least not the Western sangha. The lamas do not teach their lay students that this is part of their practice. Thus, the lay people look at Western monastics and think, "Well, who are they?" and have little sympathy or appreciation for what they are trying to do. The lamas take good care of their own Tibetan sangha. They build monasteries and train the monks. When Tibetans are ordained, they have a support system. There is a monastery they can enter and the society respects their decision to live a monastic life. For the Western sangha, this is largely non-existent. The lamas ordain people, who are then thrown into the world with no training, preparation, encouragement, support, or guidance—and they are expected to keep their vows, do their practice, and run Dharma centers. This is very hard, and I am surprised that so many of the Western monastics stay for as long as they do. I am not surprised when they disrobe. They start with so much enthusiasm, with so much pure faith and devotion, and gradually their inspiration decreases. They get discouraged and disillusioned, and no one helps them. This is true, Your Holiness. It is a very difficult situation, which has never before occurred in the history of Buddhism. In the past, the sangha was firmly established, nurtured, and cared for. In the West this is not happening. I truly do not know why. There are a few monasteries—mostly in the Theravada tradition and a few in other traditions—which are doing well, but for the nuns what is there? There is hardly anything, quite frankly.

But to end on a higher note, I pray that this life of purity and renunciation which is so rare and precious in the world, that this jewel of the sangha may not be thrown down into the mud of our indifference and contempt.

(At this point, His Holiness remains silent. He then puts his head in this hands and weeps, as the audience sits speechlessly. After several minutes, he raises his head and says, "You are quite brave.")

AUDIENCE WITH HIS HOLINESS THE DALAI LAMA

Dharamsala, India
March 4, 1996

BHIKSHUNI THUBTEN CHODRON (WHO ACTED AS THE SPOKESPERSON FOR THE NUNS):

Your Holiness, we would like to begin with a summary of *Life as a Western Buddhist Nun* and then ask some questions. In recent years, Buddhist women—nuns and laywomen from Asia and the West—have met together and become more active. We are working together to improve our situation, obtain better education and conditions for Dharma practice, and increase our ability to be of benefit and service to others. Our program, *Life as a Western Buddhist Nun*, was an educational program emphasizing the study of Vinaya. The nuns also had discussions, shared experiences, and got to know each other. The idea for this program came in the spring of 1993, after Bhikshuni Tenzin Palmo gave a presentation at the conference of Western Buddhist teachers that you attended.

There were about one hundred participants in the program. Of these, the majority was from the four Tibetan traditions. Twenty-one Tibetan and Himalayan nuns were among the participants. Three Theravada nuns, two Zen priests, and a number of laywomen also attended. Our principal teachers were two excellent Vinaya masters: Geshe Thubten Ngawang, a bhikshu from Sera Monastery, who now teaches in Tibet Center in Germany, and Venerable Bhikshuni Master Wu Yin from Luminary Temple in Taiwan.

We also received teachings from Ling Rinpoche, Dorzong Rinpoche, Bero Khentze Rinpoche, Geshe Sonam Rinchen, Khandro Rinpoche, Khenpo Choga, Bhikshu Tashi Tsering, and others. In the evenings, the senior Western nuns gave talks. On the new moon, the sixteen bhikshunis present did *posadha*, our bimonthly confession, in English, while the sramanerikas attended the Tibetan *posadha* at the Tibetan Temple in Bodhgaya.

Life as a Western Buddhist Nun was unique in many ways. First, a variety of women of different ages from different countries, backgrounds, and Buddhist traditions attended. Second, the teaching program, with its concentrated Vinaya teachings, was excellent. Such a program, which includes teachings on the bhikshuni precepts given by a bhikshuni, has never happened in this way for Western nuns before. Meditation periods and two discussion groups occurred each day. In addition, Venerable Master Wu Yin asked us to perform skits that showed through drama our situation as Western Buddhist nuns. This was a new way to learn, and many points emerged that would not have been expressed otherwise.

Your Holiness and the Private Office have continuously supported us in the entire process of our organizing and preparing this program, and we are very indebted and grateful to you for this. It could not have happened without your blessings and support

His Holiness:
I am very happy to meet all of you here and congratulate you on the success of your program. I am deeply touched and impressed by your enthusiasm and your eagerness to practice Dharma and to facilitate other people interested in Dharma practice. No matter how difficult something may be at the beginning, if we keep up our spirit and determination, our wisdom will eventually overcome all difficulties. You can make great contributions for the Buddhadharma and for the benefit of sentient beings. From our

side, we are happy to do whatever we can to contribute to making your activities successful.

Question:

When the Buddha first ordained monastics, there were no precepts. The precepts were made gradually, when certain monks and nuns misbehaved. Thus the Buddha must have had in mind a deeper meaning or purpose for monasticism, beyond the keeping of precepts. Please discuss this.

His Holiness:

On the individual level, there is a purpose in being a monk or nun, which the Buddha himself exemplified. Why did he renounce his nice life as the prince of a small kingdom? He knew that if he remained in the kingdom with all of the householder's activities, those circumstances would compel him to become attached or angry, and these are obstacles to practice. In family life, you have to engage in worldly activities to take care of your family. The advantage of being a monk or nun is that you do not have to be entrapped in too many worldly activities and distractions. You have more time to think and to develop genuine compassion and concern for all sentient beings, and this accumulates great virtues. On the other hand, with your own family, your concern and compassion are generally directed to your family and friends. Perhaps there are some exceptional cases, but generally speaking, the lay life is a real burden, and that pain is a real pain. It is difficult to accumulate virtue because one's activities are based on attachment. Therefore, becoming a monk or nun, one who is without family concerns, is conducive for practicing the Buddhadharma because the basic aim of Dharma practice is nirvana, not just day-to-day happiness. We seek nirvana, permanent cessation of samsaric suffering, so we want to pacify the factors binding us in the samsaric world. The chief of these is attachment. Therefore the main purpose of being a monastic is to reduce attachment: we work on no longer being attached to family, sexual pleasure, and other worldly enjoyments.

At the time of the Buddha, initially no monasteries existed. The Buddha and his sangha stayed wherever there was an available place or food, and for the time being that was the "monastery." When some of his monastic disciples became old or sick, he decided it was better to have permanent places where they could stay. In this way, the monastic system developed. However, the main purpose or target was still nirvana, detachment from samsaric suffering and its causes. Unfortunately, sometimes monastics make the monastery their new home and develop attachments there. In this case, one is freed from the bigger household life, but gets entrapped in the smaller "household" life. Still, comparatively, by remaining in a monastery or nunnery, you have more facilities and advantageous circumstances for Dharma practice.

Question:
We see the value and purpose of living in a nuns' community, yet our Western culture makes us very individualistic. We like to do things on our own and we have our own ideas, and this sometimes makes it difficult to form a community. Yet another part of us wants to live with other nuns in a community. Please speak to how we could work with our individualistic tendencies. Is it important to have nuns' communities for the continuation of the Dharma and the existence of the Sangha for many generations to come? What are the advantages of group practice versus individual practice?

His Holiness:
Nunneries are very important. One reason is, according to my observation, women's interest and faith in spiritual practice is generally stronger than men's. Another reason is that I think the rights of women practitioners in

the Tibetan Buddhist community have been neglected. Women have great potential, genuine interest, and heartfelt wish to practice, but due to lack of proper facilities, many sincere women have no opportunity to do so. Because of the number of sincere women, I think nunneries are at least as, if not more, important than monasteries, in order to care for women's spiritual needs.

I do not think you have to be too concerned about Westerners being especially individualistic. Tibetans are also individualistic! In every field, certain things can be achieved more easily and quickly with the effort of a community, rather than individually. We are individualistic, but at the same time, we are also social animals. It is human nature to want a sense of community, to feel there is a group to which we belong and which looks after us. Sometimes there is tension between the two: while concentrating too much on community benefit and sacrificing individual rights is one extreme, putting too much emphasis on the individual and neglecting the welfare of the community is another. I think the Buddhist concept of Pratimoksa is individualistic! Pratimoksa means individual liberation (laughs), yet as a monk or nun, we have a sense of community. If we know the reality of things more clearly, there is not much problem.

Question:
Please speak about the advantage of taking higher ordination as a bhikshu or bhikshuni. Why did you choose to become a bhikshu rather than to remain as a novice? If Western nuns wish to take bhikshuni ordination, how should they prepare for it?

His Holiness:
Generally, living in higher ordination makes all your virtuous activities more effective and powerful. The teachings of the bodhisattva vehicle and tantric

vehicle express great appreciation for the bhikshu vow, and we feel it is a great opportunity to take higher ordination. A bhikshu or bhikshuni has more precepts. If you look at them point by point, you may sometimes feel there are too many precepts. But when you look at the purpose—to reduce attachment and other disturbing attitudes—the large number of precepts makes sense. The Vinaya puts more emphasis on our actions in order to reduce our disturbing attitudes, and thus it contains very detailed and precise precepts about physical and verbal actions. The higher vows—the bodhisattva vow and the tantric vow—put more emphasis on the motivation. If we look at the main purpose, how they work, we will have a better understanding of the purpose of the many bhikshu and bhikshuni precepts.

Generally speaking, those Buddhist practitioners who are really determined to follow this practice according to the Buddha's guidance gradually take the vows of sramanera, bhikshu, bodhisattva, and finally the tantric vow. I feel the real preparation for taking bhikshuni ordination is not the study of the Vinaya, but strong meditation on the nature of samsara. For example, we have a precept of celibacy. If you just think, "Sex is not good. Buddha prohibited it, so I can't do it," controlling your desire will be very difficult. On the other hand, if you think of your fundamental aim—nirvana—you will understand the reason for the precept, and following it will become easier. When you do analytical meditation on the Four Noble Truths, you will gain conviction that the first two truths are to be abandoned and the last two to be actualized. Examining whether the disturbing attitudes—ignorance, anger, attachment, and so forth, which cause suffering—can be eliminated, you will become confident that they can and feel that attaining nirvana is your real purpose in life. You will know that there is a systematic way to reduce and finally eliminate the disturbing attitudes, and you can clearly see that an alternative exists. Then your practice of the precepts will become meaningful because you will know that it facilitates your attaining nirvana. Otherwise, keeping precepts is like a punishment. You cannot eat in the afternoon (laughs). Thus study and analytical meditation on the Four Noble Truths is the main preparation for bhikshuni ordination. I recommend gradually taking the various levels of precepts leading toward liberation: first becoming an *upasika*, then a full *upasika*, an *upasika* with celibacy, a sramanerika, a *siksamana*, and a bhikshuni.

Question:

Some lamas ordain Western women who are not sufficiently screened or prepared. Despite their having false expectations or financial or emotional difficulties, the lamas still ordain them. After ordination these nuns are left to float and do not receive proper training and support. Many of the senior Western nuns are concerned about this situation, and we would like to have more input into the evaluation, preparation, and ordination of nuns. Is this possible?

His Holiness:

This is an excellent idea. Of course we cannot immediately establish an organization that can issue orders. However, you can begin to actualize this excellent idea and start screening and preparing people wherever it is possible. If you do this well, people will gradually recognize your work, join in, and follow you. As a start, at a conference of Tibetan lamas, you could highlight the problem of people being ordained without proper evaluation. When there is the opportunity, I will talk about these things to other people. Being ordained without due evaluation and preparation occurs among the monks as well. Even tantric initiations are given without sufficient consideration. It is not good to give these to whomever asks. In the 1960s and 1970s, some Westerners who did not have proper understanding requested Tibetan lamas to give initiations, and the Tibetan lamas did not prepare them thoroughly. Thus, mistakes were made on both sides at the beginning, and now we face the difficulties that have come as a result. I think both parties are becoming more mature now, so perhaps there is less danger. It is important to pay attention to the mistakes we have committed and are committing, and to warn others so that these errors are not made again in the future.

Question:
Is there a different way of practicing the Vinaya for someone who is in the Vajrayana tradition? How do we integrate our study and practice of Vinaya with our study and practice of the tantra?

His Holiness:
We are celibate monastics and simultaneously practice the Vajrayana through visualization. For example, we visualize a consort, but we never touch one. Unless we have developed the power to control all our energy completely and have gained the correct understanding of emptiness, we do not implement practice with an actual consort. Only at a very high stage of practice does one possess all the faculties through which the disturbing attitudes can be transformed into positive energy. Thus, although we monastics practice the higher practices of the completion stage, we do so in terms of visualization. In our external behavior, we should follow the stricter discipline of the Vinaya and remain celibate. In ancient India, one of the reasons the Buddhadharma degenerated was that people incorrectly implemented certain tantric explanations.

Question:
Western nuns have a wide spectrum of lifestyles. For example, some keep

the precept of not handling money very strictly. Other nuns are forced to get a job in order to live, and this necessitates wearing lay clothes and not shaving their hair. Is this a valid, new, alternative way to be a nun in the West?

His Holiness: Obviously, we must make every effort to follow the Vinaya teachings and precepts as best as we can. In certain cases, adaptations can be made if there is sufficient reason to do so. But we should not make these adaptations too easily. First we should give preference to following the Vinaya precepts as they are. In cases where enough sound reasons necessitating an adaptation exist, then making careful adaptations are permissible.

Question:

What is the source of joy in the mind? How do we maintain a sense of joy? How do we deal with doubt and insecurity that may arise, especially when we see older sangha members disrobe?

His Holiness:

When you gain some inner experience as a result of your spiritual practice, you will have a deep feeling of satisfaction, happiness, and enjoyment. You will have a special kind of confidence that is a result of your Dharma practice and meditation. Analytical meditation is the most effective method for our mind. However, without proper knowledge and understanding, meditation is difficult because we do not know to meditate. To be able to do analytical meditation effectively, we should have broad knowledge of the structure of Buddhism. Thus, study is important, and it makes a difference in our meditation. On the other hand, sometimes in our Tibetan monasteries there is too much emphasis on the intellectual side, and practice is neglected. As a result some people are great scholars, but as soon as their lecture finishes, then ugliness appears (laughs). Why? They may intellectually be great scholars, but the Dharma is not integrated with their life. Once we personally experience some deeper value as a result of our practice, our happiness will not be affected no matter what other people say or do. Through our own experience, we will be convinced that Dharma practice is valuable. Then, even if a senior monk goes down, it will not affect us negatively, and we will feel compassion for him. However, if we lack our own deep Dharma experiences and just blindly follow others, doubt will take hold of us if those people fall. The Buddha himself made that very clear. Right at the beginning he stressed the importance of each individual taking responsibility for his or her decisions and Dharma practice. Our progress on the path depends on our own effort. Our lamas or teachers are not our creator. If they are the creator, and something goes wrong with the creator, then we also go wrong! But the Buddha's teaching is wonderful for it says that we ourselves are the creator. However, if one of your teachers falls, try not to criticize him with anger. It is better to just let it be and not pay it undue attention. There is no reason for it to disturb your own confidence. Some Westerners, and Tibetans too, rely too much on the person. That is a mistake. We must rely more on the teaching, not on the person.

GLOSSARY

action prohibited by the Buddha

An action which is not naturally negative but is to be avoided because the Buddha established a precept prohibiting it, for example, singing and dancing done with attachment by those with monastic precepts.

anagarika

A person holding the eight precepts and preparing to be a monastic.

arhat

One who is free from samsara and has attained liberation.

brahmacarya (Tibetan: *tshangs par spyod pa*)

Celibacy.

bhikshu (Pali: bhikkhu, Tibetan: *gelong*)

A fully ordained Buddhist monk.

bhikshuni (Pali: bhikkhuni, Tibetan: *gelongma*)

A fully ordained Buddhist nun.

bodhicitta

The altruistic aspiration to become a Buddha in order to benefit all sentient beings.

bodhisattva

One who has generated the spontaneous altruistic intention to become a Buddha in order to benefit sentient beings.

Buddha

A fully enlightened being. "The Buddha" refers to the historical Buddha of this age, Shakyamuni Buddha.

Dharma (Pali: Dhamma)

The Buddha's teachings; the true paths and true cessations in a realized being's mindstream.

Dharmagupta

The Vinaya school prevalent in China, Korea, Taiwan, and Vietnam.

Four Noble Truths

The Buddha's first teaching which describes our present situation and our potential: the truths of suffering, its causes, their cessation, and the path to that cessation.

geshe

    A learned master (comparable to a Ph.D.) in Tibetan Buddhism.

guru (Tibetan: lama)

    A spiritual master or teacher.

gurudhamma (Sanskrit: *gurudharma*)

    Eight important rules regarding the relationship between bhikshus and bhikshunis.

karma

    Action, either one bringing a result or a decision made by an assembly of monastics.

koan

    A seeming puzzle given by a Zen master to his or her student. By contemplating this and holding it in mind, the student comes to understand the nature of reality.

lama (Sanskrit: guru)

    A spiritual master or teacher.

maechee

    An eight-precept nun in Thailand.

Mahaprajapati (Pali: Mahapajapati)

    The Buddha's aunt and stepmother, who became the first bhikshuni.

Mahayana

    The Buddhist tradition emphasizing the development of bodhicitta and leading to full enlightenment.

Mulasarvastivada

    The Vinaya school prevalent in Tibet.

naturally negative actions

    Actions which bring suffering results whether one has a precept to abandon them or not, for example, killing, stealing, lying, and so on.

nirvana (Pali: nibbana)

    Liberation from cyclic existence.

ngondro

    Preliminary practices, such as prostrations and recitation of the Vajrasattva mantra, done before undertaking major tantric practices.

ordination

    The ceremony through which one becomes a monastic.

parajika

    Defeat or root downfall. If one commits this, one is no longer a monastic.

parinirvana (Pali: *parinibbana*)

    The time when a Buddha passes away and leaves his or her earthly body.

parmarabjung
Pre-novice ordination taken for the duration of one's life.

posadha (Pali: *uposatha*, Tibetan: *sojong*)
The confession ceremony held on new and full moon days during which Buddhist monastics purify and restore their precepts.

pravarana (Pali: *pavarana*; Tibetan: *gagye*)
The ceremony marking the end of the summer retreat (rains retreat).

Pratimoksa (Pali: Patimokkha)
Individual liberation; the code of monastic precepts leading to this liberation. The texts containing this code.

puja
An offering ceremony often chanted together in a group.

samsara
Cyclic existence, uncontrollably being reborn with a body and mind under the influence of disturbing attitudes and karma.

Sangha
An individual who has attained the path of seeing and above.

sangha
A community of four or more bhikshus or bhikshunis.

sanzen
A private meeting between a teacher and student in the Zen tradition.

sesshin
A meditation retreat.

siksamana (Pali: *sikkhamana*, Tibetan: *gelopma*)
A probationary nun.

sramanera (Pali: *samanera*)
A male novice monastic.

sramanerika (Pali: *samaneri*)
A female novice monastic.

sutra (Pali: sutta)
A discourse given by the Buddha, the text containing such a discourse.

Tantra
Vajrayana; a scripture taught by the Buddha describing the Vajrayana practice.

teisho
A Dharma talk.

Theravada

The Vinaya school prevalent in Southeast Asia and Sri Lanka.

Three Baskets of the Buddha's teachings (Skt: Tripitaka)

The categorization of the Buddha's teachings into three broad topics—Vinaya (ethical discipline), Sutra (discourses), and Abhidharma (knowledge of phenomena).

Three Higher Trainings (Sanskrit: *trisra-siksa*; Pali: *tisso sikkha*)

The higher trainings in ethical discipline, concentration, and wisdom.

Three Jewels (Triple Gem)

The Buddhas, the Dharma, and the Sangha. Taking refuge or entrusting one's spiritual guidance to these is the beginning of the Buddhist path.

upadhaya (upahayayini)

A senior bhikshu or bhikshuni who trains those newly ordained.

upasaka

A male Buddhist who has taken refuge and some or all of the five lay precepts.

upasika

A female Buddhist who has taken refuge and some or all of the five lay precepts.

Vajrayana

The Diamond Vehicle, a branch of the Mahayana in which the practitioner engages in Tantric practices involving visualization, mantra recitation, and so forth.

varsa (Pali: *vassa*, Tib: *yarney*)

The rains retreat or summer retreat during which the sangha is restricted to living in a certain area to avoid harming crops and insects prevalent during the monsoon rains.

vihara

A monastic dwelling, an early monastery.

Vinaya

The ethical discipline, precepts, and rules of training for the monastic community. The texts explaining this.

zazen

The type of meditation done in the Zen tradition.

zendo

A meditation hall.

FURTHER READING

VINAYA:

Bhikkhu, Thanissaro. *The Buddhist Monastic Code.* 1994. For free distribution, write to: The Abbot, Metta Forest Monastery, P.O. Box 1409, Valley Center, CA 92082, USA.

Chodron, Thubten, ed. *Preparing for Ordination: Reflections for Westerners Considering Monastic Ordination in the Tibetan Buddhist Tradition.* Seattle: Life as a Western Buddhist Nun, 1997. For free distribution, write to Dharma Friendship Foundation, P.O. Box 30011, Seattle, WA 98103, USA.

The Daily Requisites of Vinaya, English translator unknown. Taiwan: The Committee of Religious Affairs Fo Kuang Shan Buddhist Order, 1998.

Dhirasekera, Jotiya. *Buddhist Monastic Discipline.* Sri Lanka: Ministry of Higher Education Research Publication Series, 1982.

The Essentials of the Rules of Discipline for Sramanera and Sramanerikas. English translator unknown. Taiwan: The Committee of Religious Affairs Fo Kuang Shan Buddhist Order, 1998.

Gyatso, Tenzin. *Advice from Buddha Shakyamuni Concerning a Monk's Discipline.* Dharamsala: Library of Tibetan Works and Archives, 1982.

Hanh, Thich Nhat. *For a Future to Be Possible.* Berkeley: Parallax Press, 1993.

Hirakawa, Akira. *Monastic Discipline for the Buddhist Nuns.* Patna, Tokyo: Kashi Prasad Jayaswal Research Institution, 1982.

Horner, I. B. *Book of the Discipline (Vinaya-Pitaka).* Pts. 1-4 of *Sacred Books of the Buddhists.* London: Pali Text Society, 1983. London: Routledge & Kegan Paul, Ltd, 1982.

Kabilsingh, Chatsumarn, trans. *The Bhikkhuni Patimokkha of the Six Schools.* Bangkok: Thammasat University Press, 1991.

Kabilsingh, Chatsumarn. *A Comparative Study of Bhikkhuni Patimokkha.* Varanasi: Chaukhambha Orientalia, 1984.

Mohoupt, Fran, ed. *Sangha.* Kathmandu, Nepal: International Mahayana Institute. (P.O. Box 817).

The Profound Path of Peace, no. 12 (Feb. 1993). Write to: International Kagyu Sangha Association c/o Gampo Abbey, Pleasant Bay, N.S. BOE 2PO, Canada.

Rhys Davids, T. W. and Herman Oldenberg, trans. *Vinaya Texts.* Pts. 1-3. New Delhi: Atlantic Publishers and Distributors, 1990.

Tegchok, Geshe. *Monastic Rites.* London: Wisdom Publications, 1985.

Theravada Bhikkhuni Vinaya. Vol. 3 of *Vinaya Pitaka.* Pali Text Society.

Tsedroen, Jampa. *A Brief Survey of the Vinaya.* Hamburg: Dharma Edition, 1992.

Tsering, Tashi and Philippa Russell. "An Account of the Buddhist Ordination of Women." *Cho-Yang* 1.1 (1986): 21-30. Dharamsala: Council for Religious and Cultural Affairs.

Tsomo, Karma Lekshe. *Sisters in Solitude: Two Traditions of Monastic Ethics for Women.* Albany: State University of New York Press, 1996.

Upsak, C. S. *Dictionary of Early Buddhist Monastic Terms.* Varanasi: Bharati Prakashan, 1975.

Wijayaratna, Mohan. *Buddhist Monastic Life According to the Texts of the Theravada Tradition.* Trans. Claude Grangier and Steven Collins. Cambridge: Cambridge University Press, 1990.

Wu Yin. *Teachings on the Dharmagupta Bhikshuni Pratimoksa.* Given at *Life as a Western Buddhist Nun.* For audio tapes, write to Hsiang Kuang Temple, 49-1 Nei-pu, Chu-chi, Chia-I County 60406, Taiwan.

WOMEN AND BUDDHISM:

Allione, Tsultrim. *Women of Wisdom.* Arkana, NY: Routledge, 1986.

Arat, Paula. *Zen Nuns: Living Treasures of Japanese Buddhism.* Ann Arbor: University of Michigan, 1993.

Bartholomeusz, Tessa. *Women Under the Bo Tree, Buddhist Nuns in Sri Lanka.* Cambridge: Cambridge University Press, 1994.

Batchelor, Martine. *Walking on Lotus Flowers.* San Francisco: Thorsons/HarperCollins, 1996.

Cabezon, Jose Ignacio, ed. *Buddhism, Sexuality and Gender.* Albany: State University of New York Press, 1992.

Chang, Pao. *Biographies of Buddhist Nuns*. Trans. Li Jung-hsi. Osaka: Tohokai, Inc., 1981.

Chodron, Thubten. *Spiritual Sisters*. Singapore: Dana Promotion, 1995.

Falk, Nancy Auer. "The Case of the Vanishing Nuns: The Fruits of Ambivalence in Ancient Indian Buddhism." In *Unspoken Worlds: Women's Religious Lives in Non-Western Cultures*. Edited by Nancy Auer Falk and Rita M. Gross. Harper & Row Publishers, 1980.

Findlay, Ellison, ed. *Women Changing Tibetan Buddhism*. Boston: Wisdom Publications. (to be published).

Giac, Thich Man. "Establishment of the Bhiksuni Order in Vietnam." *Dharma Voice (Quarterly Bulletin of the College of Buddhist Studies)* 3 (1988): 20-22. Los Angeles.

Gross, Rita. *Buddhism After Patriarchy: A Feminist History, Analysis, and Reconstruction of Buddhism*. Albany: State University of New York Press, 1993.

Havnevik, Hanna. *Tibetan Buddhist Nuns: History, Cultural Norm, and Social Reality*. Oslo: Norwegian University Press, 1989.

Horner, I. B. *Women Under Primitive Buddhism*. Delhi: Motilal Banarsidass Publications, 1990.

Kabilsingh, Chatsumarn. *Thai Women in Buddhism*. Berkeley: Parallax Press, 1991.

Khema, Ayya. *I Give You My Life: The Autobiography of a Western Buddhist Nun*. Boston: Shambhala Publications, 1998.

Klein, Anne. *Meeting the Great Bliss Queen*. Boston: Beacon Press, 1995.

Mackenzie, Vicki. *Cave in the Snow*. Great Britain: Bloomsbury Publishing, 1998.

Murcott, Susan, trans. *The First Buddhist Women: Translations and Commentary on the Therigatha*. Berkeley: Parallax Press, 1991.

Norman, K.R., trans. *The Elders' Verses II Therigatha*. London: Luzac and Co. Ltd., 1966.

Paul, Diana Y. *Women in Buddhism*. Berkeley: University of California Press, 1985.

Piyadassi, Thera. *The Virgin's Eye*. Singapore: Samadhi Buddhist Society, 1980.

Rhys Davids, Caroline, trans. *Psalms of the Sisters*. London: Oxford University Press Warehouse, 1909.

Sakyadhita newletter. Past issues available from: Ven. Lekshe Tsomo, 400 Honbron Lane, #2615, Honolulu, HI 96815, USA.

Tsai, Kathryn. *Lives of the Nuns: Biographies of Chinese Buddhist Nuns from the 4th to 6th Centuries*. Honolulu: University of Hawaii Press, 1994.

Tsomo, Karma Lekshe, ed. *Buddhism Through American Women's Eyes*. Ithaca, N.Y.: Snow Lion Publications, 1995.

Tsomo, Karma Lekshe, ed. *Buddhist Women Across Cultures: Realizations*. Albany: State University of New York Press, 1999.

Tsomo, Karma Lekshe, ed. *Sakyadhita: Daughters of the Buddha*. Ithaca, N.Y.: Snow Lion Publications, 1988.

Tsomo, Karma Lekshe, ed. *Swimming Against the Stream: Innovative Buddhist Women*. London: Curzon Press, 1999.

Willis, Janice D., ed. *Feminine Ground, Essays on Women and Tibet*. Ithaca, N.Y.: Snow Lion Publications, 1989.

Women and Buddhism. Spring Wind - Buddhist Cultural Forum. Vol. 6, nos. 1-3 (1986). Toronto: Zen Lotus Society.

Yasodhara (formerly *NIBWA*) newsletter. Past issues available from: Dr. Chatsumarn Kabilsingh, Faculty of Liberal Arts, Thammasat University, Bangkok 10200, Thailand.